SPURGEON'S SERMONS ON ANGELS

SPURGEON'S SERMONS ON ANGELS

KREGEL
CLASSICS

Spurgeon's Sermons on Angels
by Charles H. Spurgeon

Copyright © 1996, 2024 by Kregel Publications

Published by Kregel Classics, an imprint of Kregel Publications, 2450 Oak Industrial Dr. NE, Grand Rapids, MI 49505.

Cataloging-in-Publication Data is available from The Library of Congress.

ISBN 978-0-8254-4894-2

1 2 3 4 5 / 28 27 26 25 24
Printed in the United States of America

Contents

1

Angelic Interest in the Gospel

Which things the angels desire to look into (1 Peter 1:12).

The apostle Peter wrote his first epistle to a persecuted people, many of whom were in great heaviness through manifold trials. The sufferings of the early Christians are something terrible even to think upon; the world has scarcely ever beheld more relentless cruelty than that which pursued the first servants of our Divine Lord and Master. Peter, therefore, when he wrote to these tried saints, sought to cheer and encourage them. What, then, did he write about? Why, about the Gospel, for there is nothing like the simple doctrine of salvation by redemption to comfort the most distressed spirits.

The chapter from which our text is taken is just as plain as the Gospel itself is. Peter here tells the elect strangers that they were begotten again "unto a lively hope by the resurrection of Jesus Christ from the dead, to an inheritance incorruptible, and undefiled, and that fadeth not away." He also reminds them that they "were not redeemed with corruptible things, as silver and gold . . . but with the precious blood of Christ, as of a lamb without blemish and without spot." In this chapter we have all the great central truths of the Gospel—election, redemption, regeneration, effectual calling, sanctification, and final perseverance. Brothers and sisters, whenever we want consolation, let us never go away from the Gospel to find it. The child of God always finds the best comfort in the things of God. If your comforts can only come to you from worldly society, it is quite clear that you belong to the world, but if you are one of God's true children, all that you want to cheer you under the heaviest trial is already provided for you in the Gospel of Christ and will speedily be applied to you by the Holy Spirit, the Comforter, if you only seek it at His hands. Peter here prescribes a

---

This sermon was taken from *The Metropolitan Tabernacle Pulpit* and was preached on Sunday evening, September 25, 1881.

remedy for lowness of spirits and for general depression. That remedy is to take a deeper interest in the things of God, to give ourselves more intensely to the consideration and contemplation of them. They are well worthy of all the thought that we can give to them, for if the prophets, those men with the grandest of human minds divinely inspired, yet had to search deeply to understand God's Word as revealed to them, there must be something in it that we shall do well to search out. If the holy angels, those mighty intelligences, do not so much see as "desire to look into" the things of God, there must be some very deep things hidden within the simplicities of the Gospel that you and I ought to search out. If we did search them out, we should be greatly cheered and comforted. Our minds would be taken off those trials that now so often vex us; we should be lifted high above them; we should not travel slowly and painfully over this rough road and have our feet cut with every sharp flint and our spirits pierced with every sore trial, but we should rise, as on eagle's wings, and ride on the high places of the earth and rejoice in the Savior who has done such great things for us. We should eat the fat things full of marrow which God has provided for those who diligently study His Word and prize it above all earthly treasures.

I am not going to say anything at this time about the high interest that the ancient prophets took in God's Word, but I shall confine myself very much to the interest that angels take in it, in order that I may stir you up to imitate their example. I want, first, to remind you that *angels take an active interest in the Gospel of our salvation,* and, secondly, to show you that *angels are eager students of it*—"which things the angels desire to look into."

Angels Take an Active Interest in the Gospel

Angels take an active interest in the Gospel of our salvation. It is true that *they are not interested in it for themselves.* They have never sinned, and, consequently, they need no atonement and no forgiveness. Doubtless, they have some sort of indirect interest in it which I will not attempt to explain just now, but certainly, as far as the Gospel brings salvation, healing, pardon, justification, and cleansing, angels do not need it. Never having been defiled, they need not to be washed, and being perfect in their obedience, they need not to be forgiven for any shortcomings. And yet they take a deep interest in the work of the Lord Jesus Christ. What, then, shall I say of the madness of those who are defiled by sin and yet have no interest in the fountain where they can be washed whiter than snow? What shall I say of the fatal folly of those who are guilty and yet take no thought about the method of pardon that God has provided in Christ Jesus His Son, our only Savior?

The angels are not even interested in the Gospel because of its rela-tion to any of their fellows, for fallen angels have no part nor lot in its provisions. When they fell from their first estate, God left them without hope forever; they abide in their rebellion against Him, waiting for the awful day when they shall receive the full recompense of their infa-mous revolt. There is no mercy for fallen spirits. See how God exercises His sovereignty; when men and angels had both sinned, He passed by the greater sinners and took up the lesser ones. The fallen spirits "he hath reserved in everlasting chains under darkness unto the judgment of the great day." Yet He looked on men, the creatures of a day, with eyes of pity and compassion and sent His Son to earth in our nature, that He might redeem us from the wrath that was justly our due. The angels have no direct interest in the death of Christ and the blood of Christ be-cause of any blessing that will come through Him to any of their former angelic companions, yet they desire to look into these things. What, then, shall I think of myself and of you, my brother, if, being saved our-selves, we take little or no interest in the Gospel as the one means of saving our fellow men? Shame upon us if we have less pity for mankind than angels have, for men are our brothers and nothing can save them but the Gospel of Jesus. Therefore, our common humanity ought to make us seek their welfare, and we ought to take the deepest imaginable interest in the things that make for the peace of their im-mortal souls.

Angels take a deep interest in the Gospel because they observe God's interest in it. That for which God cares, angels care for at once. That which grieves the Holy Spirit must be grievous to holy angels, too. And that which gladdens the heart of God must also make glad the spir-its that bow adoringly around His throne. The holy ones cry, each one to his fellow, "God is glorified in saving sinful men. Our blessed Lord and Leader went down to earth to accomplish the redemption of the fallen; therefore, let us learn all we can concerning His wondrous work, and wherever there is anything that we can do to help it on, let us stand, with outspread wings, eager to fly at the command of God."

Doubtless, *the angels also take an interest in the Gospel because they are full of love.* Those pure spirits love as surely as they live; not only do they love their God and love one another, but they also love us who were made a little lower than the angels. They have a great affec-tion for us—very much more, I imagine, than we have for them. We are their younger brothers, as it were, and we are, by reason of our flesh and blood, linked to materialism while they are pure spirits, yet they do not envy us the love of God, neither do they despise us on account of our faults and follies, though, I think, they must often wonder at us. They must sometimes be ready to ask questions concerning our strange behavior, just as two of them did when Christ had risen from the dead and Mary Magdalene was weeping. Those angels were full of joy because Christ had risen, so they said to her, "Woman, why weepest thou?" What could there be to weep about when Jesus had risen from the dead? Ah, beloved! the angels must often be astonished at us and think we are the strangest creatures that well can be, yet they love us, and therefore they take a great interest in that Gospel that promotes our highest good. They know what we too frequently forget—that nothing can make us so happy as for us to be holy and that nothing can make us holy but being washed in the blood of Jesus and being renewed by the Holy Spirit. Out of their homage to God and their brotherhood to man comes that interest which makes them desire to look into the deep things of God and His Gospel.

The angels have always taken an interest in all that concerns men. Some of them stood at the gate of Eden with a flaming sword, which turned every way, to keep our first father out should he attempt to force his way back when he had lost his right to all its joy, even as the most loving spirit in the world is still upon the side of justice and believes that God is righteous even though paradise is lost and man is doomed to eat bread in the sweat of his face. We are on man's side, but much more on God's; we say, Let God, the ever Just One, be glorified, whatever becomes of the sons of men.

After that fatal day of the Fall, the angels constantly watched over men here below and frequently spoke with one and another of them as God sent them with messages of mercy to Abraham or to Isaac or to Lot or to Jacob or to others of the human race. But there was a great day when in solemn pomp the chariots of God, which are "twenty thousand, even thousands of angels," came down to Mount Sinai when the law was proclaimed. The angels were there as the courtiers of the great King, to give additional solemnity to the declaration of the law of God. That they should have been present on that august occasion shows their interest in the sons of men.

But I like better to speak to you of their coming to announce the birth of Him of whom we sing, "Unto us a child is born, unto us a son is given." When that birth, which they had announced, took place, how gladly did they come and hover over Bethlehem's fields and sing the grand chorale, "Glory to God in the highest, and on earth peace, good will toward men." It was their intense interest in us that made them glad that our Redeemer was born. Then, as we sang at the commencement of this service—

> In all his toils and dangerous paths
> They did his steps attend,

> Oft paused, and wonder'd how at last
> The scene of love would end.

At that notable time when Jesus was tempted in the wilderness and was with the wild beasts, when the Devil had left Him, angels came and ministered to Him. They were ever near Him while He was here, always invisibly attendant upon His footsteps. You remember how there appeared to Him an angel strengthening Him when He was in His agony in the Garden of Gethsemane; it was a wondrous thing that the Son of God should have strength infused into Him by an angelic messenger. With what awestruck interest the angels must have watched our Lord upon the cross!

> As on the tottering tree he hung,
> And darkness veil'd the sky,
> They saw, aghast, that awful sight,
> The Lord of Glory die!

But glad were they to descend to His empty sepulcher and to enter it and guard the place where for awhile the sacred casket of His body had lain. They spoke to His disciples and comforted them by telling them that He had risen from the dead. All along, they took such interest in everything relating to Him because they recognized in Him the Savior of sinful men.

> They brought his chariot from above,
> To bear him to his throne;
> Clapp'd their triumphant wings, and cried,
> "The glorious work is done."

Nor is this all. We know from Scripture that they not only watched over the Savior, but *they rejoice over penitents*. The Lord Jesus has told us that "there is joy in the presence of the angels of God over one sinner that repenteth"; that is to say, there is joy in God's heart, and the angels can see it. They stand in God's presence, and they can see that God is glad, and we know that they also share that gladness. In the parable of the lost sheep, our Savior represents the shepherd calling together His friends and His neighbors and saying to them, "Rejoice with me; for I have found my sheep which was lost." So they do, I am sure; they rejoice over every rescued one that is brought home upon the shoulders of the Good Shepherd.

And, beloved, *they watch over every believing soul*. This is one of their chief offices, for "are they not all ministering spirits, sent forth to minister for them who shall be heirs of salvation?" That promise which Satan misquoted is true to every child of God: "He shall give his angels charge over thee, to keep thee in all thy ways. They shall bear thee up in their hands, lest thou dash thy foot against a stone." From what spiritual evils they guard us, it is not for me to attempt to tell, nor to try to describe how, often in midair, there are fierce fights between the demons from hell and the good spirits from heaven, or how the prince of the power of the air is baffled and driven back by Michael the archangel as he comes to take care of the living body of Christ, as once of old he guarded the dead body of Moses. Ah! we little know how much we owe to these invisible agents of the ever-blessed God. They are deeply interested in all His children. The parable tells us that Lazarus died, "and was carried by the angels into Abraham's bosom." What that expression means, I shall not attempt to explain, but I am quite sure that when we who love the Lord die, angels will have something to do with our departure and with our introduction into the world of happy spirits, and into the presence-chamber of the Lord our God. I like Bunyan's account of the pilgrims passing through the river and the shining ones meeting them on the other side and leading them up the steep ascent into the Celestial City where they see their Master's face with joy and go no more out forever.

Nor will they have done with us even then, for when we shall be with God eternally shut in and safe from all danger of falling and sinning, the angels will swell the music of our continual song, for they shall sing, "Worthy is the Lamb that was slain to receive power, and riches, and wisdom, and strength, and honor, and glory, and blessing." Yet we shall be able to sing what they cannot, "Thou wast slain, and hast redeemed us to God by thy blood out of every kindred, and tongue, and people, and nation; and hast made us unto our God kings and priests: and we shall reign on the earth."

Further, these dear attendants of our wandering footsteps here below, these patient guardians of our nightly hours, these angel guides who shall be our companions in death when wife and child and friend can go no farther with us, *these glorious beings shall learn from our lips in heaven the manifold wisdom of God.* They will cluster around us amazed and gladdened as, one by one, we stand upon the sea of glass; they will ask us to rehearse again and again the wonders of redeeming love and to tell them what conversion meant and what sanctification meant and how the power and wisdom and grace and patience of God were seen in the experience of each one of us; we shall be their joyful teachers, world without end.

Have I not proved to you that angels take an active interest in the Gospel of our Lord and Savior Jesus Christ? And may I not come back to this practical point—do you also take an active interest in the Gospel—you in whose nature Christ appeared—you sons of men—you who must be forever lost unless the precious blood of the bleeding Lamb be sprinkled upon you?

Is it nothing to you, all ye that pass by,
Is it nothing to you that Jesus should die?

It was for such as you that He died, even for the guilty sons and daughters of men, "for verily he took not on him the nature of angels; but he took on him the seed of Abraham." He took up men, not angels; shall they, then, be interested in the Gospel, and shall not you, whom it specially concerns, also be interested in it? I have already reminded you that they have no brother angels to be converted by the Gospel; they have no sister angels to be turned to God by the story of Calvary; yet they are deeply interested in the Gospel and also in us. Will not you, my fellow Christians, take a deeper interest in the work of God and in the propagation of the Gospel when your own flesh and blood must be converted by it or else must die eternally? Our sisters and brothers, our sons and daughters, our wives and husbands, possibly even our parents will perish forever unless Jesus Christ is brought to them, and they are brought to Him. What are you at, you careless professors, you who can go calmly to sleep while men and women are being damned? What are you thinking of, you who eat the fat and drink the sweet in the courts of the Lord's house and yet never show to the prisoners the way to liberty, nor tell to the dying the good news that "there is life for a look at the Crucified One," nor say to the perishing that there is salvation even for them in Christ Jesus your Lord? Up, up! I charge you, by every swift-winged angel who takes an interest in the Cross of Christ and in the salvation of men, arouse, sons of men; if you may, anyhow, be the means of saving some, be active in the service of that Savior who gave His all for you. God bless that exhortation to all whom it concerns!

Angels Are Eager Students of the Gospel

It is quite certain that *angels do not know all that is in the Gospel,* for they desire to look into it. All the Gospel is not known to them, and I do not think that it is all known to any of us. I have occasionally met with certain brethren who have professed to have the whole of the Gospel condensed into five points of doctrine, so that they could put it all into their waistcoat pocket and carry it there, and they seemed to think that they had not anything more to learn. If one tried to teach them any other truth beside what they already knew, they were angry, for they did not want to know any more. They are not like the holy angels, for they desire to look into these things. Dr. John Owen was, perhaps, the most profound divine who ever lived; yet Dr. John Owen could not know, on earth, as much about certain things as angels did. I should say that, this very day, he desires still to look into the mystery of redeeming love and the glory of Christ of which he wrote with such wonderful power. The apostle Paul had been converted many years when he wrote the epistle to the Philippians, yet in it he expressed the longing of his heart that he might know Christ. But did he not know Him? And if he did not, who did? No doubt, he felt that there was so much of Christ that he had not known that what he did know amounted to very little. I have heard the word *perfection* used very glibly by some who seemed to me to know little of its meaning, but will any sane man claim that he has attained to perfection in knowledge? To the Corinthians Paul wrote, "If any man think that he knoweth any thing, he knoweth nothing yet as he ought to know." The mystery of redemption was hidden in Christ from eternity, and it was only made known to the church or even to the angels gradually. They do not yet know everything. Concerning His second coming, our Lord said to His disciples, "But of that day and hour knoweth no man, no, not the angels of heaven, but my Father only."

The Devil also does not know everything. I am sure that Satan did not know that Christ came into the world to redeem men by dying for them, or else he would never have stirred them up to put Him to death. He would have been far too cunning for that; he would have tried, if possible, to keep Christ alive so that we might not have been redeemed by Him. The Devil does not know as much as he thinks he knows, even now, and often he is outwitted by a simple-hearted child of God who knows how to believe in God and is brave enough to do the right. Neither men nor prophets nor angels nor devils know all about the Gospel yet. They need still to go on studying and meditating and contemplating, as the holy beings before the throne of God are doing: "which things the angels desire to look into."

But, brethren, though they do not yet know all about Christ and His Gospel, *they want to know all they can.* They have many other subjects to study. There are all the worlds that God has made, and possibly they have liberty to range over them all; yet I do not read with reference to the marvels of astronomy, "which things the angels desire to look into." Angels doubtless know much more than all our scientific men do concerning the former ages of this world. They could tell much about the various formations and strata of which geologists talk, yet I do not find it recorded that the angels have any particular desire to look into those things. When God created the world, "the morning stars sang together, and all the sons of God shouted for joy." They have oftentimes admired the providential arrangements of God and praised the wise Ruler who guides all things with infinite wisdom. But now their chief contemplations seem to be fixed on Christ and His Gospel.

Just notice two or three passages of Scripture. Turn first to Exodus

25:20, where we read concerning the cherubim, who belong to one order of angels: "The cherubims shall stretch forth their wings on high, covering the mercy seat with their wings, and their faces shall look one to another; toward the mercy seat shall the faces of the cherubims be"—toward the mercy seat, as if their eyes were continually fixed upon the redemption of Christ, the propitiation wrought out by His sacrifice. In Daniel's day, these blessed spirits took the greatest conceivable interest in knowing all they could about our redemption. If you turn to Daniel 8:13, you can read what that man of God wrote: "Then I heard one saint"—or, "holy one"—"speaking, and another holy one said unto that certain holy one which spake, How long shall be the vision concerning the daily sacrifice, and the transgression of desolation?" "How long?"—that was the question that the holy ones asked long before Christ descended to earth. Read also in 12:5: "Then I Daniel looked, and, behold, there stood other two, the one on this side of the bank of the river, and the other on that side of the bank of the river. And one said to the man clothed in linen, which was upon the waters of the river, How long shall it be to the end of these wonders?" They asked again and again, "How long?" All their thoughts were concentrated upon the things of God, and they desired to look into them.

Now I want you to remember, in order that it may humble us, that *angels have very keen intellects*. I believe that they far excel us in their powers of thought, and yet, though they have learned so much about the Gospel, they do not pretend to have come any further than this, they desire to look into it. You and I, perhaps, suppose that we know all about the Gospel and that we do not need to have hours of study and thought and prayer and the unction of the Holy Spirit. Poor miserable fools! Angels, who are vastly superior to us in intelligence, have gone no further than to have the desire to learn and to know; I am afraid that many of you have not got as far as that. It is a grand thing to desire to look into these things; it proves that we already know something of their worth when we desire to know more.

Recollect, also, that *the intellects of angels have never been warped by prejudice*. There is not a man among us who is not prejudiced to some extent. Our parents warped us in one direction, and our companions have warped us another way, and we have all of us the propensity to take a one-sided view of things, even though we may be perfectly ignorant of the bias. Sometimes, this prejudice of ours prevents us from seeing clearly, but it is not so with the angels. There is no beam, nor even a mote, in the eye. Their knowledge is not infinite, but it is wonderful knowledge as far as it goes. Yet even they see not all that there is in the Gospel, for, of it, as of the love of God, it can truly be said—

> The firstborn sons of light
> Desire in vain its depths to see;
> They cannot reach the mystery,
> The length, and breadth, and height.

Then, again, *the angels have been looking into these things*. I know not what the age of the angels may be; we know nothing of any creation of angels since the creation of the world. In the long ages before man trod this earth, angels had begun to think of looking into the wonders of Gods grace, yet, after thousands of years, they do not fully comprehend the mysteries of redeeming love. Ah, my brothers and sisters, the Gospel is a boundless thing, even as your ruin was infinite and horrible beyond conception, and woe to the man who tries to make out that there is but a little hell and a little God and but little wrath of God! As surely as your overthrow was inconceivably terrible, so the designs of God for your redemption and your exaltation in Christ are inconceivably magnificent. "It doth not yet appear what we shall be." Some of us have very large expectations of what God means to make even of His creatures who are now cooped up in flesh and blood, but our highest anticipations will probably be far exceeded by the glorious reality. Even angels do not yet fully know, after all their study, what the mighty love of God has done and will yet do for us.

Do not forget, too, dear friends, that *angels are not subject to such infirmities as we are*. I know that I have forgotten a great deal more than I know, and I suppose that most of you have done the same. When we have learned a thing, we are often like people who take up a handful of water; it is soon all gone. What leaky sieves our memories are! Angels, however, have no such failure of mind. They have never sinned, and, therefore, from much of our infirmity, they must be altogether free. Yet, though far superior to us in this respect, this is the position they have reached: they stand over the mercy seat with wings outstretched and with their eyes continually fixed upon that token of the propitiation, desiring to look into it. That is where you and I also stand; if we are truly humble, we feel that this is as far as we have come as yet.

Now, let us inquire—*What are the things which the angels desire to look into?* I can only refer very briefly to them.

They are, first, the incarnation, life, and death of our Lord and Savior Jesus Christ; the way in which God could be just and yet justify the ungodly; that sacred art by which the suffering of the Law-giver made a sufficient recompense to the offended law; the wondrous power of those sufferings Godward and manward; how these sufferings have broken men's hearts and separated them from their sins; how they have given them joy and peace and have united them forever to their God.

You and I have only seen the sparkle on the surface of the crimson sea of redemption; we cannot understand the height and depth and length and breadth of the sufferings and death of Jesus Christ our Lord; so let us still desire to look into it, as the angels do.

Next, they desire to know something concerning the resurrection of Christ. "How do you know that?" you ask. Why, the verse before the one containing our text speaks of "the sufferings of Christ, and the glory that should follow." So angels love to think of Christ as risen from the dead, of Christ ascended, and of Christ yet to come in His glory. They desire to gaze into that mystery and to learn how the glorious God can become yet more glorious by taking upon Himself our nature and so magnifying His grace above all His name by redeeming fallen men and by lifting them up into communion with God.

Angels desire to look into all the mystery of human hearts—how they are fallen, how they are regenerated, how they are preserved, how they are sanctified, how they are strengthened, how they are taught, how they are perfected. There is a wonderful field for their inspection there in the work of the Holy Spirit upon the sons and daughters of Adam by virtue of the death of Christ.

And angels want also to know what God is going to do with this poor world. It is an awful problem to us, and so it is to them, I expect. Can you make this world out? Did you ever try to understand it? It is a dreadful nut for anyone to crack—all these millions of men continually dying without God and without Christ and without hope. What are to be the eternal issues of it all? How will it come out that God is glorified at the last when such multitudes perish? There are some brethren who think they know all about this mystery; they have a philosophy that explains it all. I have no such philosophy, nor do I wish to have. I sometimes found, when I was a child, that it was a pleasant thing for me to be with my father and to hear him talk even when I did not fully understand what he was talking about; so I find it a blessed thing to get near to God and to see what He is doing, even when I do not know what He is doing, for I am perfectly satisfied that He cannot do anything that is wrong. Still, angels and men may join in the common desire to look into the wonderful working of God's providence and grace.

But the angels also desire to look into the glory that shall follow. What is the glory that is yet to come to those spirits of just men made perfect who, as yet, have not their glorified bodies, but are waiting for them until the resurrection trumpet shall sound? What will be the glory of that moment when, in the twinkling of an eye, the dead shall be raised incorruptible and the living shall be changed? And what will be the glory of that dread hour when heaven and earth shall gather before the last tribunal, and on the Great White Throne the Judge shall sit, and all of woman born shall be gathered before Him to give an account of the deeds done in the body, whether they have been good or whether they have been evil? And what glory it will be, before that day has closed, when over all the world of sinners the waves of God's infinite wrath shall roll, and they shall sink to the bottom like a stone, never to taint the earth again! And what a glory it will be when all those on the King's right hand, all the blood-washed, all the redeemed, shall stream up to their everlasting thrones to sit forever with their conquering Leader and reign eternally, peers in the palace of the King, forever adoring, forever blessing His holy name! Oh, what glory will be there! I will not attempt to describe it, for even the angels, who are in heaven, desire to look into this mystery, for even they scarcely know what will be the glory of "the general assembly and church of the firstborn, which are written in heaven."

You know that the Greeks had, every now and then, a great gathering of all the nation in what they called their general assembly. Everyone was represented there—poet and philosopher, tragedian and military man. All the glories of Greece were there. Well, there is to come a general assembly, an ecumenical council of the entire church of God, and when they shall all be there on the plains of heaven—prophets, confessors, apostles, martyrs, humble men and women from every part of the world—not one of the redeemed absent, but all there with their King in the midst of them, what a shout of victory, what hallelujahs, what songs of joy, what triumphant *jubilates* shall welcome that glad day! By God's grace, I shall be there. My hearer, will you be there? Are you sure of it? If so, let the glad anticipation of it rejoice your heart even now, though you do not know what the full realization of it will be, for even angels, who have seen the lesser gatherings of the saints, have not yet seen the one universal assembly, the gathering of all the clans, the coronation of the Prince, the marriage of the bride the Lamb's wife, all the glory of God, and the splendor of the infinite meridian brilliance that will be displayed before the wondering eyes of God's elect saints and God's elect angels. They do not know what it is to be, nor do you, but we as well as they desire to look into it, and I hope we all desire to be there.

Now let me close by saying that, *as the angels are such deep students of the things of God, let us try to be the same.* I wish that I could stir up all my dear friends who are saved to try to look more closely into the things of God. I am afraid that we are going to have a greater proportion of superficial believers than we have had in the past, for we have so many people who are always hallooing about their religion. God bless them, and let them halloo as loudly as they like, but I wish that they had something more to halloo about. There are some who are always crying, "Believe, believe, believe," but, for the life of them, they could not tell you what it is that you have to believe. And many shout, "Hallelujah!" who do not know what "Hallelujah!" means, or they would be far more reverent toward that blessed word, "Praise to Jehovah!" We want, brethren and sisters, that you who are saved should seek to know how and why you were saved. You who have a hope of salvation should know the reason for the hope that is in you. Study the Scriptures much. In the Puritan days, there used to be a number of contemplative Christians who shut themselves up to study the Word of the Lord and so became masters of theology. Perhaps some were not so practical in winning souls as they ought to have been, but now we are getting to the opposite pole of the compass. We have many who are rushing about and professing to feed the people, but what do they give them? Where is your bread, sir? "Oh, I could not let these poor people wait." But why do you not go and fill your basket? You have nothing in it. "Oh! I had not time to do that; I wanted to go and give them." Give them what? Give them half of the nothing that you have brought? That will do them no good at all.

There is nothing like having good seed in the basket when you go out to sow; when you go to feed the hungry, there is nothing like having good bread to give them; that cannot be the case spiritually unless we are diligent students of the Word, unless we search the deep things of God. By all means let us advance our forces into the recesses of the Enemy's country, but let us secure our communications, and let us have a good firm basis of scriptural knowledge, otherwise mischief will come to our scattered powers. By all means be enthusiastic, by all means be intense, but you cannot keep a fire burning without fuel, and you cannot keep up real intensity and enthusiasm without a knowledge of Christ and an understanding of the things of God, "which things the angels desire to look into."

Now, dear friends, those of you who have nothing to do with this matter, I would like you to go away thinking that, if an angel cares about these things, and if an angel studies them, it is time that you did the same. I know that you are going to take your degree at the university, good sir, and I am very glad that you are likely to secure a good position in life, but I hope that you are not so foolish as to think that you know more than the angels. If they desire to look into these things, permit me to ask you to study your Bible as well as all the other classics, for this is the best classic after all. I know, dear sir, that you are a masterly thinker; you can make a great many hypotheses and pull them to pieces again. But I wish, for once, that you would consider this hypothesis—that, perhaps, you are not as wise as the angels. I should not wonder if that hypothesis should prove to be true. I have often noticed that people who rail at the Gospel do not know what it is. Many speak against the Bible, but if they were asked, "Did you ever read it?" they would have to answer, "No." He who studies God's Word is usually conquered by it; he falls in love with it and feels the power of it. So, as the holy angels desire to look into it, pray look into it yourself, good sir, and, on your looking there, may God give you to see Jesus, for all who look to Him shall be saved forever. May you be one of that blessed company, for His dear name's sake!

2

Fallen Angels a Lesson to Fallen Men

God spared not the angels that sinned, but cast them down to hell, and delivered them into chains of darkness, to be reserved unto judgment (2 Peter 2:4).

These are ancient things. Most men hunger after the latest news; let us on this occasion go back upon the earliest records and think of the hoar past, before man was made. It does us good to look back upon the past of God's dealings with His creatures; herein lies the value of history. We should not confine our attention to God's dealings with men, but we should observe how He acts toward another order of beings—how He dealt with angels before man had become the second sinner. If angels transgress, what is His conduct toward them? This study will enlarge our minds and show us great principles in their wider sweep. We shall inevitably make mistakes in our judgment as to God's conduct toward men if we do not remember sufficiently how He has dealt with beings who are in certain respects much superior to the human race. By seeing how God treated the rebellious angels, light may be cast upon His dealings with us, and thereby misapprehensions may be removed.

We shall go to our subject at once, asking aid from the Spirit of all grace. We will first view the mysterious fact of the fall of the angels and their casting away *for our warning.* Then, secondly, we shall regard the fact of the hopeless doom of the angels that sinned as it stands in contrast to the amazing mercy of the Lord toward men. Thus our second head will lead us to view the text *for our admiration,* I hope for the increase of our grateful love and reverent wonder.

This sermon was taken from *The Metropolitan Tabernacle Pulpit* and was preached at the Metropolitan Tabernacle, Newington, in 1885.

For Our Warning

"God spared not the angels that sinned, but cast them down to hell."
Behold here a wonder of wickedness, angels sin; a wonder of justice,
God spared them not; a wonder of punishment, He cast them down to
hell; a wonder of future vengeance, they are reserved to judgment! Here
are deep themes, and terrible. Black as tempest are the facts, and
flashes of terrible lightning flame forth therefrom.

Let us receive a warning, first, against *the deceivableness of sin*, for
whoever we may be, *we may never reckon that on account of our position or condition we shall be free from the assaults of sin* or even certain of not being overcome by it. Notice that these who sinned were
angels in heaven, so that there is no necessary security in the most holy
position. We know that they were in heavenly places, for it was from
that high abode that they were cast down to hell by the terrible right
hand of the Eternal King. These angels, that kept not their first estate,
but sinned against God, dwelt with their brethren in the courts of the
Most High. They seemed to be, as it were, walled around with fire to
keep out all evil from them. Their communications were only with perfect spirits like themselves; yet, as they were undergoing a probation,
they were made capable of choosing evil if they willed so to do or of
cleaving to good if their hearts were steadfast with their God. There
were none about them to tempt them to evil. They were, on the contrary, surrounded with every good and holy influence. They saw God
and abode in His courts; they conversed with seraphim and cherubim.
Their daily engagements were all of a holy order; worship and service
were their duty and delight. Their company was select; there were no
lapsed classes among them to render the moral atmosphere impure.
They were not only in a paradise but in the central abode of God
Himself. Yet evil entered into the breasts of angels—even envy, ambi-
tion, pride, rebellion—and they fell, never to rise again.

> High in the bright and happy throng,
> Satan, a tall archangel sat;
> Amongst the morning stars he sung,
> Till sin destroy'd his heavenly state.
>
> 'Twas sin that hurled him from his throne,
> Groveling in fire the rebel lies,
> "How art thou sunk in darkness down,
> Son of the morning, from the skies!"

Beloved hearer, this should teach us not to presume upon anything
connected with our position here below. You may be the child of godly
parents who watch over you with sedulous care, and yet you may grow

up to be a man of Belial. You may never enter a haunt of iniquity; your journeys may be only to and from the house of God, and yet you may be a bond slave of iniquity. The house in which you live may be none other than the house of God and the very gate of heaven through your father's prayers, and yet you may yourself live to blaspheme. Your reading may be bound up with the Bible; your companions may be of the choicest; your talk may concern holy things; you may be as if you were in the garden of the Lord, shut in to everything that is good and every evil shut out from you; yet you may have no part nor lot with the people of God. As there were a Ham and an ungodly Canaan even in Noah's ark, so may it turn out that you may be such in the very midst of all that should make you gracious and sanctified.

It is unhappy indeed to read the annals of human life and to meet with men that have gone from their mother's side—have gone from where their father knelt in prayer—have gone out from brothers and sisters whose piety was not only unquestionable but even remarkable— and they have gone to be leaders in every form of wickedness. Many of the enemies of the Cross of Christ have been so trained in godliness that we find it hard to believe that they can indeed be so vile that an apostle must declare it with tears before he is believed. The sons of God they seemed to be, but they turned out to be sons of perdition after all. Let no man, therefore, arise and shake himself as though no sins could ever bind him, because he feels himself to be a very Samson through his connections and surroundings. Yes, sir, it may be that you shall fall—fall foully, fall desperately, unless the grace of God be in you— fall so as never to come to God and Christ and find eternal life. It was so with these angels. The best natural thing that creation can work is not sufficient to preserve the fickle creature from sin: regeneration must come in—the work of the Holy Spirit, a yet higher work than the material creating power of God, or else you may put the creature where you please, and that creature may be perfect, yet sin will reach and destroy him. You and I are far from perfect. We are not angels unfallen. We are not angels at all, but we have evil hearts within us; therefore let us not imagine for a moment that the most select position can screen us from the worst of sin.

The next thought is that *the greatest possible ability, apparently consecrated, is still nothing to rely upon* as a reason why we should not yet fall so low as to prostitute it all to the service of the worst of evils. Angels are beings of remarkable power. We know that they have amazing intelligence and beauty. We read of one whose face was like that of an angel of God. When a thing is spoken of as being exceedingly good, it is often connected with angels: "Man did eat angels' food." It is supposed that everything with regard to them is of superior order and of refined quality. I suppose that a spirit that is not cumbered with flesh and blood, as we are, must be delivered from much that hampers and beclouds. Oftentimes a clear judgment is dimmed by a headache or an attack of indigestion. Anything that affects the body drags down the mind, but these angelic beings are delivered from such weakness, and they are clothed with a glory of strength and beauty and power.

Hear then and observe! However great Lucifer was, he degenerated into Satan—the son of the morning became Apollyon the destroyer. However excellent the fallen angels may once have been, they have now become potent only for mischief; their wisdom has curdled into cunning, and their strength has soured into a vicious force, so that no man may say within himself, "I am a clear thinker, therefore I shall never become a blaspheming infidel," or, "I am gifted in prayer, therefore I shall never become a blasphemer." You know not what you may become. There is a great difference between gift in prayer and grace in prayer: gift will breed pride, and pride will ensure destruction; it is only grace that can preserve to eternal glory.

There is also a great difference between office and person; therefore, a man may not say, "I am a minister: I shall be kept faithful in the church of God." Ah, me! But we have seen leaders turn aside, and we need not marvel; if angels fall, what man may think that he can stand? To trust our office as a security is to rest upon a broken reed. The grace of God can keep the least and weakest of us, but apart from that heavenly power, how dare any man hope to be preserved to the end?

Self-confidence is the beginning of declension. He that reckons that he is past temptation is already entangled in its net. We must never presume. Angels fell; why should not men? An angel occupies a high position near the throne of God: "Are they not all ministering spirits?" We have evidence in Scripture that they are called on grand occasions to discharge high commissions for the King of Kings. And yet these courtiers, these household messengers of the palace of heaven, these domestics of glory, even these went astray and fell and turned to devils. Let no man dream that because he occupies an office in the church his salvation is therefore secure—an apostle fell. The arrows of the Prince of Darkness can reach the highest seats of the synagogue. The high places of the field of service are not free from danger; no, they are the more perilous as they are the more notable. The powers of darkness make their direst onset upon the foremost soldiers of the Cross, hoping to overthrow the standard-bearers and create confusion throughout the camp.

None of us, dear friends—to continue my warning—*may suppose that we shall be kept by the mere fact that we are engaged in the sublimest possible office.* Apart from the perpetual miracle of God's grace, nothing can keep us from declension, apostasy, and spiritual death. "Oh, but I spend my time," one may say—"I spend my time wholly in the service of God! I go from door to door seeking the lost souls of men, as a city missionary," or "I conduct a large class in the school, and I have brought many to the Savior." All this is good, but if you trust in it for your standing before God, it will certainly fail you. If any one of us were to say, "But I am a minister, called to offer prayer and to preach the precious Word. My engagements are so sanctified, they bring me into such hallowed fellowship with holy things, that it is not possible that I should fall"—this would be the height of folly. We need not go beyond the pale of professed ministers of Christ to find specimens of every infamy of which man is capable. After having preached to others there is grave cause for trembling lest we be castaways ourselves. No, there is nothing in the most sacred office in the church to preserve us or our characters. Office, if we trust in it, may even become, as in the case of Judas, a Tarpeian rock from which we may be cast down to our destruction; the angelic office in heaven did not keep the angels from being hurled over the battlements of glory when once they dared to sin. Let not the angels of the churches hope to be kept from falling unless He that bears the seven stars in His right hand shall keep them even to the end.

I want you to notice, as a great warning, that *this sin of the angels was not prevented even by the fullest happiness.* Oh, what a change, dear friends, from the joy they once knew, when they were the servants of God, to being cast down to hell in chains of darkness, as they now are! The devils go about the world tempting men, but they are never released from their darkness. They cannot escape from the prison that they make for themselves—the blackness and horror of God's judgment that always shuts them in, be they where they may. What a difference between that and the throne of God and the vision thereof, which was once their joy! The service of God was once theirs, but now the slavery of evil holds them in iron bonds. Once they took delight in the high praises of their Creator, and now they curse Him in their heart of hearts. Once, on high days, when the servants of God came together, they sang for joy as they beheld new worlds created by their great Lord and King; now, everything He does is as gall and wormwood to them. They curse Him and themselves, and they are busy, occupied always in seeking to pull down His kingdom and to quench His light among the sons of men. Oh, the misery of these old offenders! They once were supremely happy, but this happiness of theirs did not suffice to preserve their fidelity.

The most golden wages will not keep a servant loyal to the kindest of masters. The most blessed experience will not preserve a soul from sinning. You may come here and be greatly blessed under a sermon and sweetly sing and pray with intense fervor and seem carried up to the gates of heaven by it, but do remember that no feelings of joy or happiness can be relied upon as sufficient holdfasts to keep us near the Lord. We have seen men drink of the cup of the Lord until they appeared to be full of love to Him, and yet they have gone back to be drunken with the cup of devils. We have known men preach the Gospel and yet afterward blaspheme every truth of revelation and deny the inspiration of the Book of God. We have known them appear to be among the holiest and the best, and yet they have come at last to be common frequenters of the most evil haunts of the city and to be ringleaders in folly. Is not this a dreadful thing, and should it not be a warning to every one of us? "Let him that thinketh he standeth take heed lest he fall." There is one who is able to keep us from falling and to present us faultless before His presence with exceeding great joy, but if we do not trust in Him and abide in Him, we shall perish. If we dare to confide in position, ability, office, service, or experience, we shall, sooner or later, discover that we are prone to sin and that when we sin, God will not spare us any more than He spared the angels that sinned.

This warning, be it noted, applies itself to the very foulest of sin. The angels did not merely sin and lose heaven, but they passed beyond all other beings in sin and made themselves fit denizens for hell. When Christ was describing the most wicked of men, He said that he was a devil. "One of you is a devil," was His expression, for the devil is the wickedest form of existence. Now, is it not singular that after being in heaven it remained possible for an angel to become so dreadful a being as a devil in hell now is? If any of us come very near to the kingdom and yet the life of God is not in us, if we are joined with the church of God and perform holy duties and yet we depend upon ourselves and so fall into sin, we may fall into the foulest of sins. I do not think that Judas could have been what he was if he had not been an apostle. The best of that which looks like goodness must be used as the raw material with which to make a traitor who will sell his Master.

The devils have gone into open war with God; the same beings that once bowed before His awful majesty are now openly and defiantly at war with the God that made them. They once could sing their chorales with delight and day without night circle the throne of God rejoicingly, but now they blaspheme and rage and rave against all that is good in earth or heaven. They go about like roaring lions seeking whom they may devour—even they who once would have been ministering spirits, eager to save and bless. They were once loyal subjects, but now they are traitors, rebels, seducers. They try to lead the people of God astray; they do their utmost to stir up sin in every human bosom. So bad have they become that their leader actually met the Son of God Himself and tempted Him to fall down and worship him. Was ever such infamous, such infernal impudence as for the Devil himself to ask the eternal Son of God to do him homage? O base proposal, that the purity of the Most High should bow itself before the impiety of a fallen spirit! Yet, so far have devils proceeded that in them evil has reached its ripeness and maturity. Let this be a lesson to us.

I must not for a moment think that apart from the keeping of God's Spirit I am incapable even of the foulest sin. Recall the story of Hazael. When the prophet told him what he would do, he exclaimed in amazement, "Is thy servant a dog, that he should do this great thing?" He was not only dog enough to seek the Syrian throne, but he was devil enough to suffocate his master with a wet cloth and then to carry out with eagerness all those terrible deeds of barbarity that the prophet had foretold. We may yet do horrible deeds that we think ourselves incapable of doing. How much of devil there lies within the unregenerate heart no man can tell. O my unrenewed hearer, I would not slander you, but I must warn you: there are all the makings of a hell within your heart! It only needs that the restraining hand of God should be removed, and you would come out in your true colors, and those are the colors of iniquity. If it were not for the restraints of society and providence, there would be eruptions of evil, even in the most moral, sufficient to shake society to its foundations.

An officer in India had tamed a leopard. From the time when it was quite a kitten he had brought it up, until it went about the house like a cat, and everybody played with it; but he was sitting in his chair one day asleep, and the leopard licked his hand—licked it in all innocence—but as he licked, the skin was broken, and the taste of blood came to the leopard, and from that moment it was not content to dwell with men. It rushed forth to kill and was no more at ease until it reached the jungle. That leopard, though tamed, was a leopard still. So a man, sobered by moral motives but unchanged in heart, is a fallen man still, and the taste of blood, I mean the taste of sin, will soon reveal the tiger in him. Wash a Russian, and you find a Tartar; tempt a moralist, and you discover a sinner! The thin crust of goodness, which is formed by education, soon disappears under temptation. You may be everything that looks like good, but except you have been born again you are still capable of the direst evil.

It does seem a horrible thing to me that there should stream from a man's lips the foulest blasphemy, and yet he that utters it was once accustomed to sing in the house of God and bow his knee with the saints. O God, that ever a creature bidding fair to serve his Maker should sink to such a depth! Yet such horrors abound! The vessel that adorned the

lordly festival is broken and thrown on the dunghill, and even so the excellent and honorable are defiled and cast away. I know what some are
whispering, "I never should become an open reprobate!" How do you
know that? You already question the warnings of Scripture, you may go
further before long. He that is the most sure is the most insecure; he
that cries, "Hold thou me up," shall be made to stand. Be this our con-
fession, "O Lord, I know that I shall become utterly vile except Your
sovereign grace prevent!" In humility let us cast ourselves upon the
mighty grace of God, and we shall be kept. In fervent earnestness let us
cry to the strong for strength, and we shall not be overcome of evil. He
that presumes shall fall; he that confides shall stand.

The text may lead us a little farther before we leave it, by giving us *a
warning against the punishment of sin* as well as against the sin itself.
Read this—"God spared not the angels that sinned, but cast them down to
hell." They were very great, they were very powerful, but God did not
spare them for that. If sinners are kings, princes, magistrates, million-
aires, God will cast them into hell. If they are commanders of all the
forces of the world, He that is a just and righteous judge would not spare
them because of their dignities and powers. "God spared not the angels,"
why should He spare you, great ones of the earth? They were very nu-
merous, too. I do not know how many there were, but we read of legions
of devils on one occasion. But God did not spare angelic sinners because
there were so many of them. He made room in hell for them all and set
them in darkness and in bonds, every one of them. God will not spare sinful men because of their millions: "the wicked shall be turned into hell,
and all the nations that forget God." Be they few or many, sinners must be
punished, and God will not turn away His wrath from those who do iniquity. God did not spare the rebel angels because of their unity. I never
heard of devils quarreling; it is very wonderful in Scripture to notice their
unanimity—their concord with one another, but "though hand join in
hand, the wicked shall not be unpunished." You unbelievers may combine
together to hate and oppose the Gospel, but it matters not; God will deal
with your confederacies and break up your unities and make you companions in hell even as you have been comrades in sin. "God spared not
the angels that sinned, but cast them down to hell."

Neither did He spare them because of their craft. There were never
such subtle creatures as these are—so wise, so deep, so crafty, but these
serpents and all the brood of them had to feel the power of God's
vengeance, notwithstanding their cunning. Men often escape at the bar
of their country because of their longheaded ways of evading the law.
They keep within legal bounds and yet are great villains. If they go over
the line, they hire a clever tongue to plead for them, be they as guilty as
they may; and through crafty pleading they escape from a righteous

sentence. Thus is it with men, but no counselors can pervert judgment with the Most High. He will deal out justice even to a hair's breadth, and He will by no means spare the guilty. "God spared not the angels that sinned"; why should He spare any guilty son of Adam? Be sure that He will not spare any one of us if we live in sin. Unless we accept the way of salvation by Jesus Christ our sin will find us out, and God will find our sin out, and He will cast us also down to the place prepared for the Devil and his angels. Let the flatterers of today preach what they may, the Lord will punish men who live and die in their sins. He spared not the angels that sinned; certainly He will not spare men if they sin. Let this stand as a warning to us.

For Our Admiration

I want you to admire, dear friends, the fact that *though angels fell, the saints of God are made to stand.* The angels sinned fatally, but the saint of God "cannot sin, because he is born of God." You know the sense in which the apostle means that, not that we do not all sin, but that we do not so sin as to depart from the living God, give up our allegiance to Him, and cease to be His loving children. No. He "keepeth himself," says the Scripture, "and that wicked one toucheth him not." But what a wonder it is! I tell you, when the tales of God's people shall be written and the records of the saints shall be read by the light of glory, we shall be miracles of grace to ourselves and to one another. "Oh," we shall say, "I had almost gone, but the hand of grace interposed and snatched me from slipping over the awful precipice. My mind almost consented to that sin, and yet I was able to cry out, 'How can I do this great wickedness and sin against God?' There was great stress of weather, and my poor boat was almost on the rocks; but still, though I grazed the bottom, yet I did not make shipwreck." Oh, if I had been left at that moment, one will say, what would have become of me? Though I had tasted of the heavenly gift and the powers of the world to come, yet, had I been left to myself at that hour, I should have so fallen that I could never again have been brought to repentance. But I was kept, preserved by as great a miracle as if a spark should fall into the sea and yet burn on or a straw should be blown into a heated furnace and should not be consumed or a moth should be trodden on by a giant and yet remain uncrushed.

> Kept alive with death so near,
> I to God the glory give.

To think that men should stand where angels fall! We are by sovereign grace called to be as near to God as the angels ever were, and in some respects we are nearer still. We are the bodyguard of Christ, His chosen ones with whom He communes. We are the table companions of our Lord; we eat of His bread and drink of His cup and are made partakers with Him. We are lifted up to be one with Him and are made to be "members of his body, of his flesh, and of his bones," yet God's eternal unbounded power keeps us in the day of temptation and leads us so that if we go through the rivers we are not drowned, and when we pass through the fires we are not burned. O the splendor of triumphant grace! Neither the glory of our calling nor the unworthiness of our original state shall cause us to be traitors. We shall perish neither through pride nor lust, but the new nature within us shall overcome all sin and abide faithful to the end.

"Now unto him that is able to keep you from falling . . . be glory and majesty, dominion and power, both now and ever." I cannot look back on my past life without feeling the tears rush into my eyes at the remembrance of how I have been preserved in the trial hour. We could not possibly tell, nor would we wish to tell in public, of those hours of weakness, those times of strong delusion, those moments of foot slipping and of heart fainting, that have happened to us. We grieve as we remember our worse than childish weaknesses. And yet we have not stained our garments; we have not dishonored the holy name by which we are named; we have not been suffered to turn aside from the straightness of our path so as to bring grief to the Holy Spirit and dishonor to the church of God. Verily this is a wonder. Mr. Bunyan tells us that Christian by the light of day looked back on the Valley of the Shadow of Death, which he had passed through in the nighttime and saw what a narrow path he had kept and what a quag there was on one side and what a miry place on the other and where the hobgoblins were and all the fiends of hell. When he looked back on it, he was lost in admiration and gratitude. So it must be and will be with you if through a dangerous way you have yet held on in your plain course and have not turned from your integrity. We shall be brimful of gratitude and love. Grace shall reign to eternal life. Redeemed men shall stand where angels fall, for God shall keep them. He is able to hold them up, and He will do it even to the end.

Now, let us learn another lesson full of admiration, and that is that *God deals in grace with men and not with angels.*

From heaven the sinning angels fell,
And wrath and darkness chained them down;
But man, vile man, forsook his bliss,
And mercy lifts him to a crown.

Amazing work of sovereign grace
That could distinguish rebels so!
Our guilty treasons called aloud
For everlasting fetters too.

Now, you that do not believe in the doctrine of election but kick at it and bite your lips at the mention of it, listen to this! God gave fallen angels no Savior, no Gospel, no space for repentance, yet He gives these to men. Why is this? What reason was there? Can you conceive one? Why did God pass the fallen angels by and yet look in love upon the sons of men? "Oh," says one, "perhaps fallen angels were the greater offenders of the two." I do not think it; certainly many men go far to rival devils in rebellion.

"Perhaps men were tempted and angels were not." Stop, let us be clear on this point. Very likely Satan, the first angel that fell, was not tempted, but just as likely all the others were. Their leader tempted them as much as Eve tempted Adam, or as the serpent tempted Eve. The mass of fallen angelhood may have been seduced by the example of Satan, the prince of devils. I do not therefore see any great difference as to that matter. This I do know, that some men are greater sinners than devils. "No," say you, "how is that?" I answer that the Devil never yet rejected free grace and dying love; the Devil never yet struggled against the Holy Spirit in his own conscience; the Devil never yet refused the mercy of God. These supreme pinnacles of wickedness are only reached by you who are hearers of the Gospel and yet cast its precious message behind your backs. Singular it is that God should deal in mercy with men who act so wickedly, while yet He never discoursed of mercy to the fallen angels nor set before them terms of peace. They were given over there and then to be bound in chains of darkness until the judgment of the last great day.

Notice that God gave the angels no respite. He did not wait for them to continue in sin for years; when they sinned, they fell. The punishment followed hard on the crime. They cast God out of their hearts, and He cast them out of heaven. How different is His conduct to some of you! You have sinned through a series of years. How old are you? Twenty years? Thirty? Forty? Fifty? Sixty? Seventy? Is it eighty years that you have lived in rebellion against God? And yet He has not cut you down! Wonderful patience! The angels He banished from His presence at once. He spared not the angels, but He has spared you. Why is this?

The Lord never entered into any parley with the angels—never invited them to repentance or to mercy. Oh, but what parleys God has had with some of you! I am not the only one who has entreated and persuaded you, but with some of you I have pleaded very earnestly that you would turn from the error of your ways and live—that you would believe in Christ and find eternal life. But why should the Lord treat concerning peace with men and not with fallen angels?

For the angels God never made a covenant of grace, "ordered in all things, and sure." They broke their covenant of works, and they fell, never to rise again. For the angels there was never a sacrifice; no dying Son of God for them, no bloody sweat and wounded hands and feet for them! And yet a great atonement is prepared for men. What sovereignty of God's grace is here displayed! He opens the golden gates of love for us and shuts the iron gate on beings nobler than we are. The Spirit of God strives with us, but He never strives with fallen angels. Devils are left to themselves, but concerning man the Lord cries, "How can I give you up?" How justly might God have left us alone for we have been given to idols, and yet He follows us with the admonitions of His mercy.

For the devils there is no pardon, no hope, no gate of heaven; yet there is all this for men. Oh, dear hearers, do not, I pray you, reject these choice gifts of almighty love. If God is so specially gracious to the race of men, let not man become singularly ungrateful to his God, presumptuously wanton in his sin. Let us turn to the Lord with full purpose of heart, seeing that He turns to us with such specialty of favor.

I am sure that it is a great wonder and a thing for admiration that God should look upon us and not on fallen angels because, as I have already said, angels certainly are not worse sinners than some men have been. Angels are not more willful than we have been, for we have sinned against light and knowledge with deliberate intent and purpose.

Angels are certainly more valuable. If God had wanted one of the two races to be employed as His servants, the best would have been chosen, and these are not men but angels. Angels can do more for God than we can, yet, He has chosen us. Angels must, surely, be more missed than men; their downfall made a great gap in heaven. We go there to fill the space and to repair the breach that was made when they were cast down from glory. But, surely, it were easier to restore the angels who came from heaven than to take up inferior creatures who had never been there. If we make a distinction between men in the distribution of our charity, we very properly say, "Let us do good to those first who would be the most miserable without it." Now, men have never known heaven and consequently cannot so much feel the loss of it as those who have been there and have fallen from it. We are like people that have always been poor, the angels have been in heaven and are therefore like wealthy persons who have come down to poverty. What a hell to them to be out of heaven! What misery to those spirits to miss the eternal glories which they once enjoyed! One would have thought, therefore, that God would have restored the angels before He upraised the human race. But He has not. He has redeemed us and left the elder race of rebels unrestored. No man knows why, and in our amazement we cry—How is this? Whence this election of grace?

Tell me, you who would leave God no choice but would deify the will of man, what all this means? Where is your proud theory that God is bound to treat all alike, as if we had a claim on God? I point you to the fallen angels, and what can you say?

Sometimes princes, when they mean to give pardon according to their will, say to themselves, "We will pardon the man who will be most dangerous if we leave him to be our enemy." Now, bad as men are and great enemies of God as they become, yet the Devil has more power to harm God than a man can have, and yet God does not pardon the Devil. He lets Satan go on with all his dreadful power and do his worst in reviling his Lord; yet the Lord's mercy comes to us whose powers are within so narrow a range compared with the fallen angels. He makes choice of puny man to receive His grace.

One would think that to restore an angel was more easy and more agreeable to the plan of the universe than to exalt fallen man. There is nothing to do but to put an angel back in his place, but men must be taken into a new existence. Christ Himself must come and be a man, to wash away the sin of man, Christ must die. Nothing more could have been needed had devils been saved. I cannot conceive the salvation of angels to be more difficult than the salvation of men. I rather conceive it to have been the easier thing of the two if the Lord had so willed it. And yet, involving as it did the incarnation of the Son of God and His death to make atonement, the infinitely gracious Father condescended to ordain that He would take up men and would not take up the fallen angels. It is a marvel. It is a mystery. I put it before you for your admiration. Oh, sirs, do not despise it! Let not such amazing sovereignty of grace be treated with contempt by any one of us. Talk no more about the injustice of the election of certain men, for if you do the devils will bear witness that you are caviling at the royal prerogative of the great Lord who says, "I will have mercy on whom I will have mercy, and I will have compassion on whom I will have compassion."

Now, I think that *I see in this a great argument with God's people*. Has the Lord given up angels and chosen you? It reminds me of that famous text, "I gave Egypt for thy ransom, Ethiopia and Seba for thee. Since thou wast precious in my sight, thou hast been honorable, and I have loved thee: therefore will I give men for thee, and people for thy life." See, He has passed angels by, and He has made choice of us; what a height of grace! Behold how He loves us! What shall we do in return? Let us do angels' work. Come, brothers and sisters, let us glow with such a fire of devotion as might have burned in an angel's heart. Let us be as intensely zealous as a redeemed angel might have been. Let us glorify God as angels would have done had they been restored and made again to taste divine favor and infinite love. What manner of people ought we to be? What manner of lives ought we to live? What manner of consecration ought to be upon us? Should not our whole beings live to God?

I have given you this somewhat in the rough, for time flies, but think it over, and profit by it. Think it over, you ungodly ones, and do not cast away mercy like this. When you read, "He took not on him the nature of angels; but he took on him the seed of Abraham," be full of surprise, and fly at once to Jesus. And, O ye saints, as ye read it, say to yourselves—

> For more love than seraphs know
> We will like seraphs burn.

God bless you, for Jesus' sake. Amen.

3

The Roaring Lion

Be sober, be vigilant; because your adversary the devil, as a roaring lion, walketh about, seeking whom he may devour: whom resist stedfast in the faith, knowing that the same afflictions are accomplished in your brethren that are in the world (1 Peter 5:8–9).

Satan, who is called by various names in the Scriptures, all descriptive of his bad qualities, was once an angel of God, perhaps one of the chief among the fiery ones—

> Foremost of the sons of light,
> Midst the bright ones doubly bright.

Sin, all-destroying sin, which has made an Aceldama out of Eden, soon found inhabitants for hell in heaven itself, plucking one of the brightest stars of the morning from its sphere and quenching it in blackest night. From that moment this evil spirit, despairing of all restoration to his former glories and happiness, has sworn perpetual hostility against the God of heaven. He has had the audacity openly to attack the Creator in all his works. He stained creation. He pulled down man from the throne of glory and rolled him in the mire of depravity. With the trail of the serpent he despoiled all Eden's beauty and left it a waste that brings forth thorns and briers, a land that must be tilled with the sweat of one's face. Not content with that, inasmuch as he had spoiled the first creation, he has incessantly attempted to despoil the second. Man, once made in the image of God, he soon ruined. Now he uses all his devices, all his craft, all the power of his skill, and all the venom of his malice to destroy twice-made man, created in the image of Christ Jesus. With ceaseless toil and untiring patience, he is ever occupied in endeavoring to crush the seed of the woman. There is no believer in Christ, no

---

This sermon was taken from the *Metropolitan Tabernacle Pulpit* and was preached on Sunday, November 17, 1861.

follower of that which is true and lovely and of good repute, who will not find himself, at some season or other, attacked by this foul fiend and the legions enlisted in his service.

Now, behold your adversary. Yes, though you cannot see his face or detect his form, believe that such a foe withstands you. It is not a myth nor a dream nor a superstitious imagination. He is as real a being as ourselves. Though a spirit, he has as much real power over hearts as we have over the hearts of others; no, in many cases far more. This is, I repeat it, no vision of the night, no phantom of a disordered brain. That Wicked One is as sternly real this day as when Christ met him in deadly conflict in the wilderness of temptation. Believers now have to fight with Apollyon in the Valley of Humiliation. Woe to the professors of godliness who are defeated by this deadly antagonist; they will find it terrible reality in the world to come. Against this Prince of Darkness we utter afresh this morning the warning of the apostle, "Whom resist stedfast in the faith."

I shall now speak to four points. First of all, *Satan's incessant activity*—he walketh about as a roaring lion, seeking whom he may devour; secondly, we will dwell awhile *upon his terrible roarings*; thirdly, *upon his ultimate aim*, seeking to devour God's people; and then, lastly, let us take up the exhortation of Peter and show *how Satan is to be overcome*.

Satan's Perpetual Activity

Only God can be omnipresent; hence, Satan can only be in one place at one time. Yet, if you will consider how much mischief he does, you will easily gather that he must have an awful degree of activity. He is here and there and everywhere, tempting us here, and anon scattering his temptations in the countries that are antipodes to us, hurrying across the sea or speeding over the land. We have no means of ascertaining what are his means of flight, but we may easily infer from his being so constantly in all places that he must travel with inconceivable velocity. He has, besides, a host of spirits who fell with him. This great dragon drew with his tail the third part of the stars of heaven—and these are ready to execute his will and obey his behests, if not with the same potency and force which belongs by hereditary right to their great leader, still with something of his spirit, his malice, and his cunning.

Think, for awhile, how active he must be! We know that *he is to be found in every place!* Enter the most hallowed sanctuary, and you shall find him there. Go where men congregate upon the Exchange, and you shall lack no signs of his being present there. Retire into the quietude of the family circle, and you will soon detect in bickerings and jealousies that Satan has scattered handfuls of evil seed there. Nor less in the deep solitude of the hermit's cave might you find the impress of his cloven foot. You shall sail from England to America and find him there amidst the clashing of swords. You shall come back and journey across the mighty empire of Russia and find him there in the tyrant's heart and perhaps, too, even in the enmity that is excited in the breasts of those who are oppressed. You shall go into the wilds where foot of Christian missionary never trod, but you shall find that Satan has penetrated into the far interior and tutored the untutored barbarian. You shall go where the name of Jesus is as yet unknown, but you shall find Satan having dominion there. He is the prince of the power of the air. Wherever the breath of life is inhaled, the poisonous miasma of temptation is a thing familiar. They that dwell in the wilderness bow before him; the kings of Seba and of Sheba offer him gifts, yes, and the dwellers in the isles acknowledge him too often as their king.

Then, remember that as he is found in all places, so *you have often found him in all your duties*. You have sought to serve God in your daily avocations, but strong temptations, furious suggestions of evil have followed you there. You have come home from your business almost brokenhearted with your slips. You have come into the family and sought to magnify your Master in the social circle, but perhaps in the best moment, when you seemed about to achieve the greatest work, you were tripped up by the heels. Your easily besetting sin overturned you, and Satan exulted at your fall. You found him there. You have said, "I will go to my bed," but in your tossings at midnight, you have found him there. You have risen and said, "I will go into my closet and shut the door," but who among us has not met the foul fiend, even there, in solitary conflict? When we wished to be wrestling with the angel of God, we have had to contend with the fiend of hell. Look upon any of your duties, Christian, and will you not see upon them marks of sin and on some not only marks of sin but marks of Satan's presence too? Satan is not in all sin; we sin of ourselves. We must not lay too much upon Satan's shoulders. Sin grows in our hearts without any sowing, just as thorns and thistles will grow in fallow furrows, but still there are times when Satan himself must have been present, and you have had to know it and feel it. On some of the old bricks of Egypt and of Babylon there has been found the mark of a dog's foot. When the brick was made, while it was left to dry, the creature passed over it and left the imprint of its foot upon it; and now, thousands of years afterward, when we pull down the wall, we find the dog mark. Thus has it been often with us. While our duties were in such a state that they were yet impressible, before they were yet sunburned and dried and ready to be built up for real practical purpose, that dog of hell has passed over them and left the dog foot on the best things that we ever did. As we look back years afterward, we perceive what we might not have seen at the time—that he really marred and stained the best performance of our most willing hands. Ah! when I think how Satan follows us in all places and in all duties, I am sometimes almost ready to apply to him the language of David when he spoke of the omnipresent God—"Whither shall I go from thy spirit? or whither shall I flee from thy presence? If I ascend up into heaven, thou art there: if I make my bed in hell, behold, thou art there. If I take the wings of the morning, and dwell in the uttermost parts of the sea; even there shall thy hand lead me, and thy right hand shall hold me. If I say, Surely the darkness shall cover me; even the night shall be light about me." But glory be to God, if I climb to heaven you are not there. There I can escape you. Beyond the reach of your roarings my spirit shall find her rest in God.

We must observe also how *Satan is ready to vent his spite against us in all frames of heart.* When we are depressed in spirit—perhaps some bodily illness has brought us low, our animal spirits have ebbed, and we feel ready to sink, then that old coward Satan is sure to attack us. I have always noted as a matter of experience that he prefers rather to attack some of us when we are in a low and weak state than at any other time. Oh! how temptation has staggered us when we have been sick! We have said, "Ah! if this had but come when I was well, then I could have caught it on the shield at once; in fact I would have laughed at it and broken it in pieces." But Satan avails himself of our sad and weak frames in order to make his fiery darts tell more effectively. On the other hand, if we are joyous and triumphant and are something in the frame of mind that David was when he danced before the ark, then Satan knows how to set his traps by tempting us to presumption—"My mountain stands firm, I shall never be moved"; or else to carnal security—"Soul, take your ease, you have much goods laid up for many years"; or else to self-righteousness—"My own power and goodness have exalted me." Or else, he will even attempt to poison our joys with the spleen of evil forebodings. "Ah!" says he, "this is too good to hold; you will soon be cast down, and all those fine plumes of yours shall yet be trodden like the mire of the streets." He well knows how, in every frame of mind, to make our condition minister to his devouring purposes. He will follow you, Christian, when your soul is all but despairing, and he will whisper in your ears— "God has forsaken you and given you over to the will of your enemies." And he will track your upward course, riding as it were on cherub's wings, when you tread the starry pathway of communion. He will dog your footsteps even upon Tabor's summit and climb with you to Pisgah's brow. On the temple's pinnacle he will tempt you, saying, "Cast yourself down," and on the mountain's highest peak he will attack you with, "Bow down and worship me."

And ah! remember how well *he knows how to turn all the events of providence to our ill.* Here comes Esau, hungry with hunting; there is a mess of pottage ready, that he may be tempted to sell his birthright. Here is Noah, glad to escape from his long confinement in the ark; he is merry, and there is the wine cup ready for him, that he may drink. Here is Peter; his faith is low, but his presumption is high, and there is a maiden ready to say—"Thou also wast with Jesus of Nazareth." There is Judas, and there are thirty pieces of silver in the priestly hand to tempt him, aye, and there is the rope afterward for him to hang himself withal. No lack of means! If there be a Jonah, wishing to go to Tarshish rather than to Nineveh, there is a ship ready to take him. Satan has his providences, as if to counterfeit the providence of God. At least, he knows how to use God's providence to serve his own ends.

One of the greatest mercies God bestows upon us is His not permitting our inclinations and opportunities to meet. Have you not sometimes noticed that when you had had the inclination to a sin, there has been no opportunity, and when the opportunity has presented itself, you have had no inclination toward it? Satan's principal aim with believers is to bring their appetites and his temptations together—to get their souls into a dry, seared state, and then to strike the match and make them burn. He is so crafty and wily with all the experience of these many centuries that man, who is but of yesterday, can scarcely be thought of as a match for him. Did he not drag down the wise man, even Solomon, whose wisdom was more excellent than any of the sons of men? Did he not lay the royal Preacher, like a helpless victim, at his feet? Did he not cast down the strong man, Samson—who could slay a thousand Philistines, but who could not resist the dallyings of Delilah? Did he not bring down even the man after God's own heart by a most sorrowful fault? Let us sorrowfully remember that we have hardly met with a perfect and an upright man against whom Satan has not vented his spleen and over whom Satan has not in some degree triumphed.

Well, I have thus spoken of Satan's terrible activity, of his following us into all places and attending us wherever we may go. I am sure that no Christian heart here thinks this to be a mere trifle. Of course there are skeptics. There are some who will not believe in the existence of this evil spirit. Too generally I have noticed that when a man has no devil, he has no God. Usually when a man does not believe there is a devil, it is because he never experiences his attacks and probably never will, for the devil does not take the trouble to go and look after those he is sure of. "Oh! no," he says, "let them take their ease; I do not need to tempt them." But I say this, if a man has ever met Satan, as John

Bunyan describes Christian meeting Apollyon in the Valley of Humiliation, he will have no doubt of the existence of a devil.

When I have stood foot to foot with the archtempter in some dire hour of conflict, I could no more doubt his being there struggling and wrestling with my soul than could a soldier who has been cut and scarred and wounded, while bleeding and faint, doubt that there must have been an antagonist to inflict those wounds. Experience will be to man, after all, the best proof of this, and we cannot expect that those who have never known the joys of the Holy Spirit will know much about the attacks of the Evil Spirit, nor that those who doubt that there is a God, can ever be much tormented with the Devil. "Oh!" says Satan, "let them alone, they will fall into the ditch of themselves; there is no need that I should go abroad after them." I think I remember telling you of Mr. Beecher's illustration. When the servant went out with his master to catch wild ducks, one of the ducks being a little wounded, the master made the most desperate efforts to get that, but he observed that when it was dead and had fallen down, he did not trouble much about it, because he could pick it up at any time. And so it is with dead souls; the Devil can pick them up at any time. It is those that are wounded but have got some little life that he is afraid of losing. Such as these he is sure to pursue; he will be ever striving to get them safe in his grasp.

Satan's Roarings

The destroyer has many ways of mischief. Here in the text he is compared to a roaring lion. In some passages of Scripture you will remember he is compared to a fowler. Now, a fowler makes no noise. It would altogether defeat his end if he were to frighten the birds; as quietly as possible he sets his lure, and with sweet notes he seeks to enchant his victim until it is taken in the trap. That is quite a different thing from the roaring lion of the text. In another passage it is said that he knows how to transform himself into an angel of light, and then, plausibly and smoothly, he teaches false doctrine and error and all the while appears to have a holy zeal for truth and the most earnest love for that which is delicate and lovely and of good repute.

We have plenty of specimens in these days of the Devil teaching morality. You sometimes take up a newspaper of the skeptic or scorpion school, whose writers hate all true religion as much as the Devil hates virtue, and you find a most unctuous article upon the indelicacies of some honest preacher or a very pious lamentation over the presumed follies of an earnest minister. Never let the Devil accuse Christians of cant and hypocrisy again; let him find his answer in his own dear allies who can plead for the sanctity of places that they abhor and for a solemnity that they despise. Of all devils the most devilish is the saintly hypocrite, loving sin and yet pleading against it in order to promote it. In this text, however, he is not an angel of light but a roaring lion. I think it was Rutherford who said that he liked the Devil best in this shape. I remember in one of his letters he thanks God that He had given him a roaring Devil to deal with. Now what is the peculiar temptation that is intended under the metaphor of a roaring lion—again we repeat it—not the slouching gait of a prowling lion who is seeking after its prey and will only roar when it gives its spring, but a lion that roars until he makes the very forests startle and shakes the hills which gird the prairie.

Those roarings of Satan are threefold. Perhaps Peter here alluded to *the roaring of persecution.* How Satan roared with persecutions in Peter's days! He roared and roared and roared again, until none but stout hearts dared to show themselves valiant for Christ. There were the underground prisons filled with frogs and serpents and toads, where breath or fresh air never chased away the noxious smell and pestilential vapor. There were racks and gibbets; there was the sword for beheading and the stake for burning; there was dragging at the heels of the wild horse; there was smearing over with pitch and then setting the body, still alive, to burn in Nero's garden. There were torments that must not be described, the very pictures of which are enough to make one's eyes weep blood as you look upon them. There was nothing for the Christian then but banishment and imprisonment; these were the lowest penalties. "They were stoned, they were sawn asunder; . . . they wandered about in sheepskins and goatskins; being destitute, afflicted, tormented."

Those were the roarings of the lion in good Peter's day. Since then, from his old den at Rome, what roarings has he given forth, like thunders indeed to all except the men who knew the difference between the mimic thunders of hell and the real thunders of the God of heaven! Let Smithfield testify to the roarings of this lion! Let our cemeteries and graveyards, which still bear the memorial of our myriad martyrs, testify how the lion has roared at us! And let our denomination especially, persecuted alike by Protestant and Romanist, hunted both by good and bad upon the face of the earth—let the thousands that have been drowned in the rivers of Holland and Germany—let the multitudes who have there been put to the most exquisite torture merely because they would hold God's holy ordinance and would not prostitute it at will of the pope or prelate—let all these speak and tell how Satan has roared in days of old! He has not half the roar in him now that he had then! Why, he can do nothing at all against us! His roars nowadays are like the hissings of some angry cat. All he can do is but to use cruel mockings, now and then a wicked slander or a jeer or a caricature or a witty sentence. What are these? Oh! if we cannot bear these, what should we have done when the lion used to roar in real lionlike style? Well, well, he may growl again before some of us have yet gone off the face of the earth, for we know not what may happen. But let him roar; we know, blessed be God, that He who is for us is more than all they that be against us.

But there is another kind of furious attack, *the roaring of strong and vehement temptation.* This some of us have felt. Do you know what it is, Christian—I hope you do not—do you know what it is sometimes to be caught hold of by the clutch of some frightful temptation that you hate, loathe, detest, and abominate, and yet the clutch of the hand is seconded by an arm so terrific in its strength that it drags you right on against your will. You look at the sin, look it in the very face; you feel you cannot do this great wickedness and sin against God, and yet the impulse, strong and stern, mysterious and irresistible, drags you on until you come to the edge of the precipice and look down upon the yawning gulf, which threatens to swallow you up quick, and in the last moment, as by the very skin of your teeth, you are delivered, and your foot does not slip, neither do you fall into the hand of the destroyer; yet you have had reason to say—"My feet were almost gone; my steps had well nigh slipped." Have you known what it is to have this temptation come again and again and again, until you were in a very agony? You felt that you had rather die than thus be perpetually assaulted, for you feared that in an evil hour you might leave your God and turn to perdition.

You have been like good Mr. Standfast in Bunyan's *Pilgrim;* when tempted by Madam Bubble, he fell at last down upon his knees, and with sighs and cries to God he begged Him to deliver him, and He that comes to the help of the feeble at last delivered His servant. Have you ever known this? This is one of Satan's roarings at you, thrusting his temptation against you like the torments to which they put some of the early martyrs when they laid them down and poured filthy water down their throats in such immense quantities that they were at last killed. Though they loathed the filthy liquid, yet their enemies continued to pour on and on. So has Satan done with us, pouring down his filth, cramming us with his mire, constraining us as much as possible to yield to temptation.

My peculiar temptation has been constant unbelief. I know that God's promise is true and that He that said it will do it. He that has performed of old changes not and will be firm and faithful even to the end. Yet does this temptation incessantly assail me—"Doubt Him; distrust Him; He will leave you yet." I can assure you when that temptation is aided by a nervous state of mind, it is very hard to stand day by day and say, "No, I cannot doubt my God; He that has been with me in days gone by is with me still; He will not forsake His servant, nor put him away." That perpetual assaulting, that perpetual stabbing and cutting and hacking at one's faith is not so easy to endure. O God, deliver us, we pray, and make us more than conquerors by Your Spirit's power!

Once more, Satan has another way of roaring. I do not suppose that one in ten of God's people knows anything about this—and they need not wish to—Satan can *roar also in the Christian's ears with blasphemies.* I do not allude now to those evil thoughts that spring up in the minds of men who, in their childhood and their early youth, went far into sin. I know that you will sometimes, when in prayer, be troubled with the snatch of an old song that you once were used to singing, and perhaps, when you would be most free from every unhallowed thought, some coarse expression which you heard in your former haunts will return again and again and again. Why, the verse of a hymn may suggest to you some unholy thing, or a text of Scripture bring up some of those old recollections that you have longed to forget.

But I allude now more especially to those yet more ferocious attacks of Satan when he will inject blasphemous thoughts into the minds of believers who never thought such things before. You know how Bunyan describes it. "Good Christian had to pass through the valley of the shadow of death. About the midst of this valley, he perceived the mouth of hell to be: and just when he was come over against the mouth of the pit, one of the wicked ones got behind him, and stepped up softly to him, and whisperingly suggested many grievous blasphemies to him, which he verily thought had proceeded from his own mind. This put Christian more to it than anything he had met with before, even to think that now he should blaspheme Him that he so much loved before. Yet, if he could have helped it, he would not have done it. But he had not the discretion either to stop his ears, or to know from whence those blasphemies came."

Seldom does the ministry allude to these matters, but, inasmuch as they trouble some of the people of God, I believe it to be the duty of a faithful shepherd of the flock to minister to those who are called to pass through this dark and dismal state. Oh! the horrors and terrors that Satan has sometimes caused to God's people by the thoughts that were not theirs but proceeded from himself or from some of his fiends! First, he suggested the thought so vividly that they cried with David— "Horror hath taken hold upon me because of the wicked that forsake thy law"; then, when the thought had flashed for a moment upon the soul, he gave a second horror by saying, "Ah! you are not a child of God or you would not have so vile a nature," whereas you never thought of it at all. It was his suggestion, not yours, and then, having laid his sin at your door, he has turned accuser of the brethren and has sought to cast down your faith from its excellency by making you imagine that you had committed the unpardonable sin. Now, if he roars against you either with persecution or with temptation or with diabolical insinuations, take the language of our apostle here—"Whom resist steadfast in the faith, knowing that the same afflictions are accomplished in your brethren that are in the world."

Satan's Ultimate Aim

Nothing short of the total destruction of a believer will ever satisfy our adversary. Nothing less than the perfection and complete salvation of a Christian is the heart's desire of our Savior. He will never see the full fruition of the travail of His soul until all His people are completely saved. The reverse is true of Satan. He can never be content until he sees the believer utterly devoured. He would rend him in pieces and break his bones and utterly destroy him, if he could. Do not, therefore, indulge the thought that the main purpose of Satan is to make you miserable. He is pleased with that, but that is not his ultimate end. Sometimes he may even make you happy, for he has dainty poisons sweet to the taste that he administers to God's people. If he feels that our destruction can be more readily achieved by sweets than by bitters, he certainly would prefer that which would best effect his end.

> More the treacherous calm I dread
> Than tempests rolling overhead,

said Toplady; much in the same spirit, said a Puritan divine of old— "There is no temptation so hard to bear, as not being tempted at all." Indeed, it is a stern temptation to be left at ease. When we think we have no occasion for our swords, we begin to unbuckle them from our sides; we strip off our armor plate piece by piece, and then we become most exposed to the attack of our enemies.

Satan will be glad enough, no doubt, to see your faith weakened, but his aim is to destroy that faith so that you may not believe in God to the saving of your soul. He will be pleased enough if he can throw mire into the eyes of your hope so that you can no more look to the goodly land that is beyond Jordan, but he will never be satisfied until he puts those eyes out altogether and sends you, like Samson, to grind at the mill. Let us take this for our comfort: if it be Satan's desire that we may be utterly destroyed, in that at least he is certain to be defeated. When it comes to a question which shall win the victory, Christ, the Eternal Son of God, or Satan, the prince of the power of the air, we need have no doubt as to which shall succeed. If the battle were between Satan and man, then, indeed, woe worth the day to us! We might quit ourselves like men and be strong, but before this giant all the host of Israel must flee. But the battle is not ours; it is the mighty God's. He that once broke this serpent's head still wages war with him. Yes, and Christ

Himself must be defeated, the glory of His Cross must be dimmed, His arm must be broken, the crown of sovereignty must be snatched from His head, and His throne must reel beneath Him before one of those for whom He died and on whom He set His love should ever be cast away or be given up to the power of His adversary. In this, then, tried believer, count it your joy that he may worry, but he cannot rend; he may wound, but he cannot kill; he may get his foot upon thee to make a full end of thee, but thou shalt yet start up with fresh strength and say, "Rejoice not against me, O mine enemy: when I fall, I shall arise; when I sit in darkness, the LORD shall be a light unto me."

How Satan Is Overcome

What should we do in order that we may overcome this adversary? *Resist steadfast in the faith.* This is our first defense. When Satan attacks us as an angel of light, we need not so much resist by open antagonism as by flight. There are some temptations that are only to be overcome by running away from them, but when Satan roars, we must raise the shout and the war cry. To run *then* would be cowardice and must entail certain destruction. Suppose now that Satan roars with persecution, (and it is a poor roar that he can raise in that way now!), or, suppose you are slandered, vilified, abused—will you give way? Then are you undone. Will you say, "No, never, by Him that called me to this work, I will see this battle out, and in the name of Him who has been my helper hitherto, I set up the banner and cry, Jehovah-Nissi; the Lord of hosts is our banner; the God of Jacob is our refuge." You have done well; you have resisted, and you will win the day.

Has he assailed you with some temptation obnoxious to your spirit? Yield an inch, and you are undone; but become more watchful and more vigilant over yourself in that particular sin, and resistance must certainly bring victory. Or has he injected blasphemy? Resist. Be more prayerful every time he is more active. He will soon give it up if he finds that his attacks drive you to Christ. Often has Satan been nothing but a big black dog to drive Christ's sheep nearer to the Master. Often has he been like a tremendous crested billow that has just lifted the poor shipwrecked mariner onto the rock, and from very fear has made him cling the more tightly there. If he thrusts you thus, match him by turning even his temptations to good account, and he will soon give up that mode of warfare and exchange it for another. Resist him.

But how resist him? "Steadfast in the faith." Seek to obtain a clear knowledge of the doctrines of the Gospel and then get a good grip of them. Be ready to die sooner than give up a particle of God's revealed truth. This will make you strong. Then take hold of the promises of God which are *yes* and *amen* in Christ Jesus. Know that to every doctrine there is some opposite promise. Have ready for every attack some strong word commencing with "Is it written?" Answer Satan with, "Thus saith the Lord"—stedfast in the faith." Remember, all the water outside of a ship cannot sink it. It is the water inside that perils its safety. So if your faith can keep its hold, and you can still say, "Though he slay me, yet will I trust in him." Satan may batter your shield, but he has not wounded your flesh.

> Amidst temptations sharp and long,
> My soul to this dear refuge flies;
> Hope is my anchor, firm and strong,
> While tempests blow, and billows rise.
>
> The gospel bears my spirits up;
> A faithful and unchanging God
> Lays the foundation for my hope,
> In oaths, and promises, and blood.

The conflict may be long, but the victory is absolutely sure. Oh, poor soul! do but keep near to the Cross and you are safe. Throw your arms around the dying Savior. Let the droppings of His blood fall on your sins, and even if you cannot see Him, still believe Him. Still say, "I know that He came into the world to save sinners, of whom I am chief, and I will cling to the sinner's Savior as my only hope and trust." Then let Satan roar, he cannot hurt; let him rage, his fury is vain. He may but show his teeth, for he certainly cannot bite. "Whom resist steadfast in the faith."

But there is another word added for our comfort—"knowing that the same afflictions are accomplished in your brethren that are in the world." This is well sketched by John Bunyan in that picture I have already alluded to of the Valley of the Shadow of Death. "As Christian was going along the exceedingly narrow pathway, with a deep ditch on one side, and a dangerous quag upon the other, he came to a stand, and he had half a thought to go back; and then again he thought he might be halfway through the valley; so he resolved to go on. And while he pondered and mused, he heard the voice of a man as going before him, saying, 'Yea, though I walk through the valley of the shadow of death, I will fear no evil, for thou art with me.' Then he was glad, and that for these reasons. He gathered from thence that some who feared God were in this valley as well as himself; that God was with them, though they perceived him not; that he hoped to have company by-and-by. So he went on, and called to him that was before, but he knew not what to answer for that he also thought himself to be alone."

Here honest John hits our experience in life. It is likely enough that as I am speaking this morning, some of you will say, "I did not think that anybody else ever felt as I feel." And though I tell you these things and know that many of you have heard Satan roar, I am compelled to confess that I have frequently said in my own heart, "I do not believe that any other man ever had this temptation before me. "Well, this text stands to refute our supposition, "The same afflictions are accomplished in your brethren that are in the world." Martin Luther was wont to say that next to Holy Scripture, the best teacher for a minister was temptation; he put affliction next, but temptation he kept first in his view.

When we have been tempted and tried ourselves, we know how to succor others. I grant you it is hard to have the conviction on your mind when you are standing in a perilous place where never man stood before and you are tempted as never man was tempted before you. Come, believer, we will talk this matter over for two or three seconds. Certainly your Lord has been there before, for He was tempted in all points like as you are. Scripture says that all your brethren have had some participation in your trials. Now mark, as they suffered, as you suffer, no temptation has overtaken you but such as is common to man. As they came through the temptation safe and unharmed, so shall you. As they testified that their light afflictions worked out for them a far more exceeding and eternal weight of glory, so that shall be your testimony. As they have overcome and now circle the throne of God clothed in pure white garments, so will you. And inasmuch as their temptations have left no scars upon their brows, no stains upon their robes, no rent in their royal mantles, so neither shall Satan be able to disfigure or to mutilate you. You shall come out of every trial and every struggle losing nothing therein save that which it is well to lose—your dross and your tin, your chaff and your bran. You shall come forth from the deep waters washed, cleansed, and purified. God grant that so it may be with you, but it can only be so by your resisting Satan, steadfast in the faith.

And now, I am addressing some this morning whom the precept does not reach, for they have no faith in which to stand fast. If you know what a blessed thing it is to be a Christian, you would weep your eyes out that you are not Christians yourselves. "Oh!" say you, "but you have described to us the temptations of Satan!" Just so, but it is a blessed thing to be a Christian in his very worst state. As I look sometimes upon those pictures that are drawn by the artist to illustrate the *Pilgrim's Progress*, even when I have seen poor John up to his neck in the mire, I have thought I would sooner be Christian in the Slough of Despond than Pliable on the dry land on the other side; sooner be Christian when the dragon hurled all his darts at him, though he smiled not all the day long—sooner be Christian then than be Hypocrisy or

Formality climbing over the wall to go some other way. It is a good thing to be a Christian even in his very worst state, and what must it be in his best? Young men and young women, as one of your own age, I bear my testimony that to follow Christ is the most blessed and pleasant thing, even in this present evil world.

> I would not change my bless'd estate
> For all the world calls good or great;
> And while my faith can keep her hold,
> I envy not the sinner's gold.

But who am I, that I should say this? Why, nothing but a poor miserable sinner who looks for all in Christ. With nothing in my hand, I simply cling to His Cross. Nor am I an inch forwarder than I was twelve years ago in this respect. My cry then was, "None but Jesus, none but Jesus," and it is my cry now and shall be my cry even to the end. And what are you today but a lost, guilty sinner? But do not despair. Trust Jesus! Trust Jesus—and the joys and privileges of the Christian are yours. Now, this moment cast yourself on Him. Look to His agony and bloody sweat, His Cross, His passion, His death, His burial, His resurrection, His ascension, and you shall find a balm for every fear, a cordial for every distress. All that you want and all that your heart can ever desire is most surely to be found in Christ Jesus your Lord.

May God grant us to be partakers of that grace that is in His most blessed name, that we may not be destroyed by the destroyer!

4

The Angelic Life

For in the resurrection they neither marry, nor are given in marriage, but are as the angels of God in heaven (Matthew 22:30).

We must all of us develop one way or the other. Manhood, as we see it here, is but the green blade or, at the best, the corn in the ear; the full corn in the ear will only be seen in the world to come. We must either descend or ascend; none of us can remain in the position that he occupies today. Some are sliding every hour downward, descending by the force of evil habits. More and more do they become the serfs and slaves of the Devil and by consequence, more and more developed into his image and they find their doom written in these words, "Depart . . . into everlasting fire, prepared for the devil and his angels." You followed Satan, you grew more and more like him, and now receive the heritage appointed for him. On the other hand, he who by repentance and faith is brought into the fellowship of the Gospel receives grace upon grace; he advances from glory to glory in a more perfect resemblance to heavenly beings, and, at the last, angels having rejoiced over his repentance, angels to whom he had become like carry his soul into the bosom of God. Which shall it be with you, man? Will you ripen for the golden sickle and for the harvest home of heaven, or will you blacken for the scythe of iron that shall mow you down, to be bound up in the bundle with your fellows and consumed as tares? One or other it must be. O may infinite grace overcome our natural tendencies, and may we be among those who go from strength to strength, until they ascend into the hill of the Lord and are made like to the angels.

Without further preface, the subject of this morning's discourse will be *in what respects the life of spirits before the throne is like to that of*

This sermon was taken from *The Metropolitan Tabernacle Pulpit* and was preached on Sunday morning, November 22, 1868.

angels; and then, secondly, we may have, perhaps, *a few practical thoughts about the commencement of the angelic life while yet here below.*

How Saints Are Like Angels

In what respects are those saints who have passed the stream of death like unto the angels? The likeness, though it lies in many points, more or less prominently may be seen, I think, distinctly in five particulars.

1. The saints of God are like to the angels as to *the qualities of their persons.* In one matter they always were alike, namely, that both angels and saints are creatures of God and must by no means be looked upon in any higher light. A false church has commanded its votaries to pay religious homage to angels, contrary both to the example and the express precept of Holy Writ. The angels are no more to be adored than saintly men, and neither the one nor the other can be worshiped without incurring the sin of idolatry. Take two parallel cases. When John, seeing an angel and taking him for his Lord, bowed down to worship him, the answer was, "See thou do it not: I am thy fellowservant . . . worship God." When the heathen at Lystra brought forth bullocks and sheep and were about to do sacrifice to Paul and Barnabas as to Mercury and Jupiter, these holy men rent their clothes and declared that they were men of like passions with others. Angels and holy men refuse all kinds of worship; they unanimously sing, "Not to us, not to us, but to the name of Jehovah be all the praise." Oh! the longsuffering of God in tolerating that apostate and accursed church which has dared to set up both saints and angels, men and women, and I know not what besides as objects of reverence in rivalry of the Lord of Hosts.

That is but incidental, however. The saints of heaven are like the angels in their persons in the fact that sex is forever obliterated there. "They neither marry nor are given in marriage"—from which I do not gather that so much as may be spiritual in the feminine character or anything that is mental in the masculine character will be destroyed but that in the bodily frame all that which divided the sexes will be no more. I imagine that saints before the throne may some of them exhibit that exquisite tenderness, that heroism of affection, that will indicate them to have been holy women here below, and that other spirits in their special force and vigor, courage and zeal, may reveal, even in glory, the fact that in the church militant they were among the valiant men of Israel. Why not? Yet all else that is carnal in male and female must be gone, and we shall be one in Christ Jesus in whom there is neither male nor female. Marriage will be out of the question.

This is linked with a further likeness, namely, that the spirits above are like to angels in their immortality. They cannot die. Such a thing as a funeral knell was never heard in heaven. No angel was ever carried to his grave, though angels have been in the sepulcher for there sat two, at the head and the feet, where the body of Jesus had lain; they were visitors, not dwellers there. There is nothing about angels upon which the death worm can feed; no sepulcher could encase their free spirits, and the bonds of death could not hold them for a moment. So is it with the freed ones who have passed through the grave and are now with Christ—they cannot die. Ages upon ages may roll on; eternity's ceaseless cycles may continue, but there shall be no gray hairs of decay upon the heads of the immortals; celestials shall never decay. For this reason, therefore, the population of yonder realms needs never to be repaired by births. Here it is a perpetual struggle: life contending with death, death marking its universal victory and scarring the face of the earth with tombs, but life triumphant still, ever sending little children to gather flowers above the graves. The flood of life, though apparently drunk up by the Behemoth of death, still rolls on, a broader and deeper torrent than before. Therefore are they like the angels in heaven, since there is no death and consequently no necessity of birth to repair the waste of population.

We have reason to believe, also, that since these spirits before the throne are like the angels, even when the resurrection trumpet shall be sounded and the spirits, disembodied for a time, shall be again clothed upon, they shall be like the angels in the fact of the maturity of their beings. In heaven babes will be no longer babes. He who was a babe here shall be fully developed there. Neither shall there be in heaven the weary old man tottering on his staff; he shall not carry there his failing eye and trembling knee; he shall be in the glory of his purified manhood and shall feel no decay. The child shall be as though he were a hundred years old, and the aged man shall wear more than the honors of his youth. I read not of angels either as youthful or waxing old. They stand ever in a blessed perfection, and so shall the saints of God ever be both physically and spiritually. "Thou hast the dew of thy youth," O Jesus, and that same dew falls upon all the plants of your right-hand planting. We suppose, too, that all the spirits before the throne are like angels in the matter of their beauty. The disembodied saints are fair in the eyes of Jesus, even as they are, and when their spiritual bodies shall rise all radiant with "the glory of the celestial," then shall their comeliness be seen of all.

"It is sown in dishonor," says the apostle; "it is raised in glory." Whatever of dishonor there might have been in the uncomely feature of the poor creature whom we committed to the earth, there shall be no deformity to mar the countenance of the nobler thing that shall rise from the sepulcher at the bidding of God. "It doth not yet appear what we shall be," but that we shall be lovely beyond expression is most certain, for "we shall be like him; for we shall see him as he is." There will be a glory about risen saints that will even transcend the glory of angels, for to them He has never said that they should be made like to the Only Begotten. But this is the portion of all the blood bought and blood washed, that they be fashioned in the likeness of Christ, when they shall see Him face-to-face.

As we shall resemble the angels in beauty, so no doubt we shall also equal them in strength: "Bless the LORD, ye his angels, that excel in strength." Thus saith the apostle, "It is sown in weakness; it is raised in power." What kind of power that will be we may guess. There will be an enlarged mental capacity, a far more extensive spiritual range. So far as the new body is concerned, there will be an amount of power in it of which we have no conception. What we shall be, beloved, in the matter of strength, we cannot tell, but this we know, that we shall not need so constantly to stretch our weary frames upon the bed of rest and to lie half our time in unconsciousness, for we shall serve Him day and night in His temple; this indicates a degree of alertness and physical endurance to which we are total strangers now. We shall in this also be as the angels of God.

Just then for a minute let your thoughts foresee that blessed personality that shall be yours when this present age is past. You suffer today; you are today despised and rejected. But as from yonder creeping caterpillar or from this dried up chrysalis there will arise a lovely creature with wings colored like the rainbow, so from your poor groaning humanity there shall come forth a fair and lovely being. Your spirit also shall cast off the slough of its natural depravity, be rid of all the foulness and damage of its sojourn here below, your whole man shall be restored a goodly fabric—a temple glorious to look upon in which God shall dwell with you and in which you shall dwell with God.

2. Now, secondly, there will be a likeness between the angels and glorified saints in *the matter of character*. "Thy will be done in earth, as it is in heaven" teaches us that angels do the will of God perfectly, cheerfully, instantly, unweariedly, with the highest possible alacrity. So do those blessed spirits to whom it is given to see Jehovah's face; it is their delight to do the will of their Father who is in heaven. Whatever the Lord may charge them to do, it is their heaven to perform, for in heaven the will of the Lord is the will of His people. Here below, my brethren and sisters, to will is present with us, but how to perform that which we would we find not. We would be holy, but we find another law in our members warring against the law of our minds. We sigh and cry by reason of the sin that dwells in us until we say, "O wretched man that I am! who shall deliver me from the body of this death?" But angels know not what it is to be fallen; they have never fought with any

temptations from within, though once assailed by the great temptation from without by which Satan and his followers fell from happiness. They carry about with them no inbred sin. They find no heavy clay to clog their celestial ardors; they have not to lament lascivious desires or covetous cravings; they have no proud thoughts that must be cast down, no depressions of spirit, no tauntings of unbelief, no motions of self-will. They serve God without a slur in their obedience. No thought of sin ever taints their soul; no syllable of evil ever falls from their holy lips; no thought of transgression defiles their service.

So is it with the saints who dwell in glory with them. They too are without fault before the throne of God. They have washed their robes and made them white in the blood of the Lamb. The Spirit of God, like a refining fire, has purged out of their nature everything that is evil, and they are this day as pure as God Himself in the righteousness of Christ and in the inwrought purity that is the work of the Holy Spirit. Do you not long to be with them, if it were only for the sake of this purity—for deliverance from sin will be an escape from all sorrow, and the obtaining of perfect holiness will be the climax of delight. Oh, if we could but perfectly serve God, we would make no conditions about place! Perfection in a dungeon were infinitely better than the least sin in a palace. If one could be quite delivered from all evil and it were possible that such a spirit could suffer physical pain, yet the joy of being rid of sin would make amends for all the torment that could possibly be heaped upon the body. Brethren and sisters, this portion is yours and mine. Fighting today with sin against deadly odds and often tempted to fear that we shall be defeated, we may rest assured that we shall conquer through the blood of the Lamb. Yonder is the crown—let your faith grasp it. Persevere courageously, for all things are possible to him that believes. The most inveterate habit may be broken; the lust that overcame us yesterday shall overcome us no more if we rest in the power of the indwelling God and in the might of the reigning Savior. Only be of good cheer, for through Jesus you shall overcome, and the crown shall be yours, world without end.

3. Thirdly, the souls of the blessed are like to angels as to *their occupation*. Angels, we read, bend around the throne in sacred worship. They cast their crowns before the throne upon the glassy sea and worship the Lamb forever and ever. There is never a moment, whether earth is swathed in light or clothed in darkness, in which the Son of God is not adored by ten thousand times ten thousand of these celestial spirits. Cherubim and seraphim veil their faces before the everliving Son of God. Worship is their perpetual avocation. Even so is it with all those whom Christ has redeemed with blood. They too are forever worshiping. To Jesus they pay their perpetual love. The elders are

represented as standing before the throne with their vials full of odors sweet and their golden harps representing the perpetual and acceptable praises of the glorified church. Oh, how sweet worship often is on earth, but what must it be in heaven! We love our Sabbaths, and the place of our assembling becomes very dear to us because it is no other than the house of God to our souls, but oh, to worship perfectly, without distracting thoughts and wandering minds—how blessed will it be! Such service is to be our portion soon.

Angels are described in Scripture as being occupied in holy song. John heard the voice of an innumerable company of angels. They join in the strain that goes up before the throne, ascribing honor and glory and majesty to the Lamb once slain. In this selfsame chorus the glorified spirits eagerly unite and even sweeter is their note, for angels cannot praise the Lord Jesus for having washed them in His blood, and this is the loudest of all the notes. The blood washed contribute peculiar richness to the strain as their joyous hearts lift up the chorus, "Worthy is the Lamb! for He was slain, and hast redeemed us to God by His blood! The Lord shall reign forever and ever." Oh, that heavenly song! Would that some stray notes would visit my ears even now, that I might learn how to speak thereof! Hear what John says of it: "And I heard a voice from heaven, as the voice of many waters, and as the voice of a great thunder: and I heard the voice of harpers harping with their harps: and they sung as it were a new song before the throne, and before the four beasts." Glory be to Christ today, though we cannot join in the seraphic song as we would desire, we send up our contribution of heartfelt praise to Him that lives and was slain.

In addition to adoration and praise, we have much reason to believe that angels spend their existence in a wondering study of the ways of God, especially of God's gracious acts. "Which things," said the apostle, "the angels desire to look into." That they are not perfect in knowledge is quite certain, for "of that day and that hour knoweth no man, no, not the angels which are in heaven." They are continually increasing in knowledge, and it appears from the book of Daniel that they ask questions and long to be instructed. That vision that Jacob saw in which the angels of God were ascending and descending upon the ladder pictures to us the contemplations of divine spirits who are ascending and descending in meditation upon Jesus, studying the glories of the incarnate God, His descending into the tomb, and His triumphant ascent to His Father's throne. Their contemplations are constantly hovering about the Cross and the doings of the incarnate God. Such surely will be the occupation of the blessed. The difficulties today that stagger us will be explained to us in heaven. What you know not now, you shall know hereafter. Mysteries too deep for our present plumb line will yield up their treasure to us in another state, for here we know in part, but there shall we know even as we are known. Truths but dimly guessed at and perceived in shadow shall be seen in clearer light—"for now we see through a glass, darkly; but then face-to-face." Scholars in Christ, how will you grow in knowledge there! You loving students of the inspired page, how will you revel in divine teachings there! The best of commentaries shall be the Author's own explanation. He who wrote the Scriptures shall be with you, and you shall ask Him, "What do you mean by this dark saying?" Or, perhaps, we shall get altogether beyond the letter and, needing no more the words and sentences, shall feed on the opened Spirit, the celestial meaning of the heart of God. Certainly we shall be like the angels, since our studies will be all absorbed in devout and divine things.

The angels of heaven gaze upon the face of God. This is a scriptural expression, not mine, for our Lord says that "in heaven their angels do always behold the face of my Father which is in heaven." And what must that be? Brethren, you are not to give a carnal meaning to these words, as though God could be seen with eyes either angelic or human, for He is not to be seen with these dull optics. God is a spirit, and spirit only discerns God by thought and mental apprehension; but what an apprehension of God that must be which is intended by the expression, "They do always behold the face of God"! Moses, the master spirit of the old dispensation, asked to see God, but he was only indulged with a sight of what our version calls His back parts, but which should more fittingly be described as the flowing train, the skirts of the Almighty's splendor. This was all he could see, though his eye was more strengthened than that of any man under the legal dispensation. But, brethren, we in heaven, like the angels, shall see His face, and His name shall be in our foreheads.

> Father of Jesus, love's reward,
> What raptures will it be,
> Prostrate before thy throne to lie,
> And ever gaze on thee!

Still we have not exhausted the occupations of the angels. These that I have already mentioned are rather contemplative—worship, song, study, and beatific vision—but the flaming ones above have occupations that are connected with earth. For instance, they feel sympathetic joy. We should not have known this if Jesus had not said, "There is joy in the presence of the angels of God over one sinner that repenteth." I believe this, that the souls of men redeemed will have the same kind of joy, and I can imagine the soul of the believer rejoicing over the child that was left unconverted, saved after its parents' ascent into heaven—saved through the prayers that a mother left behind her, bequeathing them upon her dying bed as her best and most sacred legacy. Many fathers have seen their posthumous spiritual children born to them through prayers they offered on earth, not fulfilled until after the prayer had been exchanged for praise. I sometimes think—it may be fancy—that if in glory I ever shall withdraw my eye from the sight of my Lord, if ever I may stay the song to my Well-beloved for a moment, it shall be to gaze over the battlements of heaven to see how the church on earth among which I labored may be prospering. Surely those venerated men who aforetime ministered to this flock must feel a peculiar joy in our prosperity, and as the news is telegraphed from earth to heaven that hundreds have been born to God and that the Word among us has been quick and powerful and sharper than any two-edged sword, if the angels rejoice, I cannot believe but what the glorified spirits, far more akin to repenting sinners than angels are, must have a yet deeper sympathy and feel a yet more exultant mirth.

Still, I must pass on. Angels are engaged in heaven, we are told, in untiring service. Gabriel flies at his Lord's word, whether it is to Mary or to the shepherds or to the king. It matters nothing to the angel whether he descends to smite the hosts of Sennacherib or to be the guardian of a little child. It has been well said that if two angels were dispatched to earth and the one were to rule an empire amidst all terrestrial splendor and the other were to perform the drudgery of a scullion, the angels would have no choice, so long as they knew their Lord's mind. Whichever God wills, they will. For those bright spirits consider not themselves, but only the good pleasure of their God. We little know what they do for us. There is a wondrous guardianship exercised secretly by them over all the seed royal of heaven. They are always engaged; they are never idle. They are never to be found where Satan offers mischief still for idle spirits to perform, but day without night they serve their God.

Lastly on this point, they are constant attendants at the courts of heaven. Wherever Jesus is, we have the angels round about Him. "When he cometh in the glory of his Father with the holy angels." When the prince moves, the courtiers go with the king. Wherever the king may be, there are the gentlemen-at-arms, and there are his bodyguards; so wherever King Jesus is, there are His angels. "The chariots of God are twenty thousand, even thousands of angels: the Lord is among them." The great King immortal and eternal, who girds His sword upon His thigh and rides out to battle, goes not forth alone; legions of angels follow at His feet. When He makes war against the Devil and his angels, all these, His watchers and holy ones, the flaming cherubim and fiery seraphim, are at His right hand like veteran bands.

Such shall be the engagements of each glorified soul. We know not what may be our sacred tasks in yonder skies—it were vain for us to surmise—but we shall not be idle, for it is written, "They . . . serve him day and night in his temple." I have thought that as angels are but the servants, they are sent out of doors to do the Master's fieldwork in the far-off portions of the universe, but we, who are His children, shall serve Him day and night in His temple at home; for is it not written, we will "dwell in the house of the Lord for ever"? Ours shall be housework, home service in the immediate presence. We shall be like that angel who stood in the sun; we shall dwell forever in the full blaze of the presence of the infinite God. We shall be equal to the angels and made like to them then, in the respect of occupation as well as in that of character and person.

4. Lest I weary you, I will add but a few words on the fourth point, though I think it a very important one. We shall be like the angels *in heavenliness*. Here we come to the vital meaning of the text. They are not married or given in marriage; they have other things to think of and they have other cares and other enjoyments. They mind not earthly things but are of a heavenly spirit. So is it with the blessed spirits before the throne. To eat and drink, to be clothed—these are things that fret their minds no more. To keep the house, to maintain the children, to thrust the wolf from the door—such anxieties never trouble celestial spirits. Brethren, this is one of the things that makes the great change so desirable to us, that after death our thoughts, our cares, our position, our desires, our joys will all be in God. Here we want externals; here we seek after carnal things, for we must eat and drink and be clothed and housed. Here we must be somewhat hampered by the grosser elements of this poor materialism, but up yonder they have no wants like our own. They consequently have no desires of an earthly kind—their desires are all concerning their God. No creature drags them downward. They are free to bow before the Creator and to think alone of Him; to

> Plunge into the Godhead's deepest sea,
> And bathe in his immensity.

Oh, what a deliverance that must be because if now for a minute or two we soar to sublimer things and climb as upon the top of Pisgah to look down upon the world, we are called to descend again into the valley amid the noise and dust of the battle, but there forever and ever we shall abide in the loftiness of heavenly things, absorbed with the glory that shall then be revealed.

5. Lastly, when we are in glory we shall be like the angels as to *our happiness*. The bliss of angels and the glorified is complete. They possess always the divine approval—this is a fountain of joy. They

know they have complete security—this is another wellspring of peace. They have suitable engagements with which to occupy their existence—and this is a wellhead of happiness. They have unbroken rest; yes, their service is rest, and rest is bliss. They have great capacities for knowing and understanding and enjoying, and an enlarged capacity, well filled with so grand a subject, ensures perpetual felicity. We shall be such. My words would utterly fail, and therefore I shall not attempt to describe the bliss of heaven. Whatever it may be, it will be ours if we are believers. Least of all the family, yet believing in the precious blood, it is yours; for it is said not of some but of all, they "are as the angels of God in heaven."

Now, unhappily for me, my time is nearly gone, and I wanted to enlarge upon the second head. The subject is too large for a single sermon. I must, therefore, give you an outline of what might have been said of the second part.

The Angelic Life on Earth

If we are to be like the angels of God in heaven, it will be well to have an outline of it here—to give ourselves to the commencement of angelic life even here. We ought to do so. Our Lord is called an angel. He is the Angel of the covenant—we ought to be like Him now; therefore, we ought to have a present resemblance to angels. Ministers are especially called to this, for this is one of their names. John writes to the angels of the seven churches. Ministers are the messengers of God to the sons of men. They should be like that angel who flew in the midst of heaven, having the everlasting Gospel to preach to every creature, and, as the angel sounded that trumpet, so, as often as the time comes and the assembly is gathered together, the Christian minister should have his trumpet ready, and that trumpet should give no uncertain sound. That we may be like angels here below is a certain fact, for we read of Stephen that his face shone, and even they who stoned him saw him as an angel of God. Why should we not be like angels, for did not men in the wilderness eat angels' food, and may we not spiritually live on angels' meat today? May we not sing—

> Never did angels taste above,
> Redeeming grace and dying love.

Yet these are the daily meat and the daily drink of all the saved souls.

We can be like angels in our occupations. First, be it ours, as it was theirs, *to declare the Word of God*. We read of the Word published by angels; we read of the angels flying through the midst of heaven with the everlasting Gospel. Men and brethren, according to your ability, be like the angels of God in this, and publish abroad the plan of salvation.

Each man of you, according to his ability, tell to others the salvation of Jesus Christ. You will never be more angelic than when God makes you the messengers of His Holy Spirit to the hearts of men.

Be it ours to imitate the angels in *fighting a good fight* while we are here. We read that Michael and his angels fought against the dragon and his angels, and the dragon was cast down. The fight is going on every day. Michael is the Lord Jesus, the only Archangel. We, like Him, and under Him, must stand as champions for the truth, never to surrender, but prepared to suffer, even to blood, striving against sin. With undaunted courage and a conscience that cannot be violated, let us stand fast for the one Lord, the one faith, and the one baptism, until He shall come who shall call us to the reckoning and shall say, "Well done, good and faithful servants." Like angels, then, let us teach, and like angels fight for the cause and for the crown of Christ.

Ours, too, let it be like angels to *oppose the way of rebels*. When Balaam was on his road to attempt to curse Israel, an angel stood with a fiery sword and made him pause. How often may a good man do that with the ungodly! Wicked men have frequently felt in the presence of gracious spirits that they could not speak profanely nor sin desperately. A good man's presence has cast an awe over the whole company. You ought, by your example, to say to the world, "Rebel not against God." Even if you speak not with your tongue, the eloquence of your life should be a constant check upon the aboundings of sin.

Not content with this, let it be ours to be the means of *setting free those who are the prisoners of hope*—God's prisoners. The angel came to Peter, smote him on the side, knocked off his chains, opened the gate, and led him out into the street. May you and I do this to some of those who, under conviction of sin, are smarting and suffering but have no liberty. Go you today, if you have opportunity, and try to smite some sleeper on the side and speak an earnest word; say to him, "Why do you sleep with death and judgment so near?" When you see him aroused, bid him follow you, as you shall open door after door of gracious promise to him and bring him into the wide street of liberty in Christ by a simple faith. You can all be angels of this kind. You need not be preachers. If you find out the disconsolate, you may bring them to Jesus in the house as well as in the great assembly.

And, then, beloved, let us also imitate the angels in our *ministering comfort to those who are saved*. When Elijah was faint under the juniper tree, an angel appeared to him and pointed to a cake that was baked upon the coals. An angel said to Paul when he was on shipboard, "Fear not." Often have angels visited godly men with this message, "Fear not." O you that love the Lord and are happy in Him yourselves, be angels in this—comfort others with the same comfort wherewith

God has comforted you this day. This very day there may be sitting near you some weeping Hannah who needs a message from God which can only come to her poor broken heart through your lips. Tell others of the goodness of God as shown in your experience. Bear your witness to the goodness and loving-kindness of the Shepherd who fails not His flock, and in this way you shall be angels of mercy to tens of thousands if the Lord spare you and give you opportunity.

We may imitate angels in another respect—namely, that we may always be *watching over souls.* You Sunday school teachers ought always to be angels. Do we not read of the little ones whom Christ took into His arms and said, "Take heed that ye despise not one of these little ones; for . . . in heaven their angels do always behold the face of my Father"? Sunday school teachers, this is your mission—see that you act it out. Angels bear us up in their hands, lest at any time we dash our foot against a stone. "The angel of the LORD encampeth round about them that fear him." Believers, learn to camp round about your fellow Christians. Help to save them from temptation and sorrow. Bear up in your hands of sympathy such as you can assist. Take away the stumbling block from the way of any who are apt to fall; bear them up in your hands lest they dash their feet against a stone. You can thus be angels of God here below.

In addition to all this, is it not written, "Bless the LORD, ye his angels"? "Let all the angels of God worship him"? Well, then, you can be like the angels now by being always in a state of praise. Let no murmur escape your lips; let no complaining dwell on your heart. Praise God, though the sun shines not; praise Him though the mists and fog are thickening; praise Him though the winds should howl and the rain descend. You are not to be ruled by circumstances. Angels praise Him in the night as well as in the day—do you the same.

> Praise him while he lends you breath,
> And when your voice is lost in death
> Let praise employ your nobler powers.

Thus have I set before you the attainments to which we shall come and the opportunities we have even now by the Holy Spirit's effectual power of forestalling those attainments. May you be desirous of beginning the angelic life; remember, the door to it is at Christ's Cross. Go where angels gaze with wonder, and gaze you with repentance. Go with your eyes full of tears for sin, and trust in Him who died for sinners, and the Lord of angels shall be your Lord, and the palace of angels shall be your home forever and ever. Amen.

5

Mahanaim, or Hosts of Angels

And Jacob went on his way, and the angels of God met him. And when Jacob saw them, he said, This is God's host: and he called the name of that place Mahanaim (Genesis 32:1–2).

And it came to pass, when David was come to Mahanaim, that Shobi the son of Nahash of Rabbah of the children of Ammon, and Machir the son of Ammiel of Lodebar, and Barzillai the Gileadite of Rogelim, brought beds, and basons, and earthen vessels, and wheat, and barley, and flour, and parched corn, and beans, and lentils, and parched pulse, and honey, and butter, and sheep, and cheese of kine, for David, and for the people that were with him, to eat: for they said, The people are hungry, and weary, and thirsty, in the wilderness (2 Samuel 17:27–29).

Let us go even unto Mahanaim and see these great sights. First, let us go with Jacob and see the two camps of angels, and then with David to observe his troops of friends.

God's Invisible Agents

Jacob shall have our first consideration.

What a varied experience is that of God's people! Their pilgrimage is over a shifting sand; their tents are ever moving and the scene around them ever changing. Here is Jacob at one time contending for a livelihood with Laban, playing trick against trick in order to match his father-in-law, then he prospers and determines to abide no more in such servitude; he flies, is pursued, debates with his angry relative, and ends the contention

---

This sermon was taken from *The Metropolitan Tabernacle Pulpit* and was preached on Sunday morning, June 20, 1880.

with a truce and a sacrifice. This unseemly family warfare must have
been a very unhappy thing for Jacob, by no means tending to raise the
tone of his thoughts or sweeten his temper or ennoble his spirit. What a
change happened to him when the next day, after Laban had gone, Jacob
found himself in the presence of angels. Here is a picture of a very different kind: the churl has gone and the cherubs have come; the greedy
taskmaster has turned his back, and the happy messengers of the blessed
God have come to welcome the patriarch on his return from exile. It is
hard to realize to the full the complete transformation.

Such changes occur in all lives, but, I think, most of all in the lives
of believers. Few passages across the ocean of life are quite free from
storm, but the redeemed of the Lord may reckon upon being tossed
with tempest even if others escape. "Many are the afflictions of the
righteous." Yet trials last not forever; clear shining comes after rain.
Change works ever. We pass from storm to calm, from breeze to hurri-
cane; we coast the shores of peace, and anon we are driven upon the
sandbanks of fear. Nor need we be surprised, for were there not great
changes in the life of our Lord and Master? Is not His life as full of
hills and valleys as ours possibly can be? We read of His being baptized
in Jordan and there and then visited by the Spirit, who descended upon
Him like a dove—then was His hour of rest. Who can tell the restful-
ness of Jesus' spirit when the Father bare witness concerning Him,
"This is my beloved Son"? But we read directly afterward, "Then was
Jesus led up of the Spirit into the wilderness to be tempted of the devil."
From the descent of the Holy Spirit to dire conflict with the Devil is a
change indeed! But another change followed it, for when that battle had
been fought out, and the triple temptation had been tried upon our Lord
in vain, we read again, "Then the devil leaveth him, and behold, angels
came and ministered unto him." In a short space our Lord's surroundings had changed from heavenly to diabolical, and again from satanic to
angelic. From heaven to the manger, from walking the sea to hanging
on the cross, from the sepulcher to the throne—what changes are these!
Can we expect to build three tabernacles and tarry in the mount when
our Lord was thus tossed to and fro?

Beloved, you will certainly find that the world is established upon the
floods and is therefore ever moving. Never reckon upon the permanence
of any joy; thank God, you need not dread the continuance of any sorrow. These things come and go and go and come; you and I, so far as we
have to live in this poor whirling world, must be removed to and fro as a
shepherd's tent and find no city to dwell in. If this happen not to our
habitations, it will certainly happen in our feelings. From of old "the
evening and the morning were the first day," and "the evening and the
morning were the second day"—the alternation of shade and shine, of

setting and rising, are from the beginning. Dawn, noon, afternoon, evening, darkness, midnight, and a new morning follow each other in all things. So must it be; there is a need for clouds and showers and morning glories, "until the day break, and the shadows flee away," when we shall be fitted to bask in the beams of everlasting noon.

In the case before us we see Jacob in the best of company—not cheated in Mesopotamia, but honored in Mahanaim; not trying to outwit Laban, but gazing upon celestial spirits. He was surrounded by angels, and he knew it. His eyes were open so that he saw spirits who in their own nature are invisible to human eyes. He became a seer and was enabled by the inward eye to behold the hosts of shining ones whom God had sent to meet him. It is a great privilege to be able to know our friends and to discern the hosts of God. We are very apt, indeed, to realize our difficulties and to forget our helps. Our allies are all around us, yet we think ourselves alone. The opposition of Satan is more easily recognized than the succor of the Lord. Oh, to have eyes and hearts opened to see how strong the Lord is on our behalf.

Jacob had just been delivered from Laban, but he was oppressed by another load: the dread of Esau was upon him. He had wronged his brother, and you cannot do a wrong without being haunted by it afterward. He had taken ungenerous advantage of Esau, and now, many, many years after it his deed came home to him, and his conscience made him afraid. Notwithstanding that he had lived with Laban so long, his conscience was sufficiently vigorous to make him tremble because he had put himself into a wrong position with his brother. Had it not been for this, he would have marched on to his father Isaac's tent with joyful foot. Dreading his brother's anger, he was greatly distressed and troubled. These angels came to bring him cheer by helping him to forget the difficulties round about him, or to lose his dread of them by looking up and seeing what defense and succor awaited him from on high. He had but to cry to God, and Esau's four hundred men would be met by legions of angels. Was not this good cheer? Have not all believers the same? Greater is He that is for us than all they that are against us.

If this morning I shall be enabled by the Holy Spirit to uplift the minds of the Lord's tried people from their visible griefs to their invisible comforts, I shall be glad. I beg them not to think exclusively of the burden they have to carry, but to remember the strength that is available for the carrying of it. If I shall cause the timorous heart to cease its dread and to trust in the living God who has promised to bear His servants through, I shall have accomplished my desire. The Lord of Hosts is with us, the God of Jacob is our refuge, and therefore no weapon that is formed against us shall prosper, and even the archenemy himself shall be bruised under our feet.

In treating of Jacob's experience at Mahanaim we will make a series of observations.

First, *God has a multitude of servants, and all these are on the side of believers.* "His camp is very great," and all the hosts in that camp are our allies. Some of these are visible agents, and many more are invisible, but nonetheless real and powerful. The great army of the Lord of Hosts consists largely of unseen agents, of forces that are not discernible except in vision or by the eye of faith. Jacob saw two squadrons of these invisible forces which are on the side of righteous men. "The angels of God met him," and he said, "This is God's host: and he called the name of that place Mahanaim [two camps]," for there a double army of angels met him.

We know that *a guard of angels always surrounds every believer.* Ministering spirits are abroad protecting the princes of the blood royal. They cannot be discerned by any of our senses, but they are perceptible by faith, and they have been made perceptible to holy men of old in vision. These bands of angels are *great in multitude*, for Jacob said, "This is God's host." A host means a considerable number, and surely the host of God is not a small one. "The chariots of God are twenty thousand, even thousands of angels." We do not know what legions wait upon the Lord, only we read of "an innumerable company of angels." We look abroad in the world and calculate the number of persons and forces friendly to our Christian warfare, but these are only what our poor optics can discover; the half cannot be told us by such means. It may be that every star is a world thronged with the servants of God who are willing and ready to dart like flames of fire upon Jehovah's errands of love. If the Lord's chosen could not be sufficiently protected by the forces available in one world, he has but to speak or will, and myriads of spirits from the far-off regions of space would come thronging forward to guard the children of their king. As the stars of the sky, countless in their armies are the invisible warriors of God. "His camp is very great." "Omnipotence has servants everywhere."

These servants of the strong God are all filled with power. There is not one that faints among them all; they run like mighty men; they prevail as men of war. A host is made up of valiant men, veterans, troopers, heroes, men fit for conflict. God's forces are exceedingly strong; nothing can stand against them. Whatever form they take, they are always potent. Even when God's host is made up of grasshoppers, cankerworms, and palmerworms, as in the book of Joel, none can resist them, and nothing can escape them. They devoured everything; they covered the earth and even darkened the sun and moon. If such be the case with insects, what must be the power of angels? We know that they "excel in strength" as they "do his commandments, hearkening unto the voice of his word." Rejoice, O children of God! There are vast armies upon your side, and each one of the warriors is clothed with the strength of God.

All these agents work in order, for it is God's host, and the host is made up of beings that march or fly, according to the order of command. "Neither shall one thrust another; they shall walk every one in his path." All the forces of nature are loyal to their Lord. None of these mighty forces dreams of rebellion. From the blazing comet which flames in the face of the universe to the tiniest fragment of shell which lies hidden in the deepest ocean cave, all matter yields itself to the supreme law that God has settled. Nor do unfallen intelligent agents mutiny against divine decrees but find their joy in rendering loving homage to their God. They are perfectly happy because consecrated; full of delight because completely absorbed in doing the will of the Most High. Oh, that we could do His will on earth as that will is done in heaven by all the heavenly ones!

Observe that in this great host *they were all punctual to the divine command.* Jacob went on his way, and the angels of God *met* him. The patriarch is no sooner astir than the hosts of God are on the wing. They did not linger until Jacob had crossed the frontier, nor did they keep him waiting when he came to the appointed rendezvous, but they were there to the moment. When God means to deliver you, beloved, in the hour of danger, you will find the appointed force ready for your succor. God's messengers are neither behind nor before their time; they will meet us to the inch and to the second in the time of need. Therefore let us proceed without fear, like Jacob, going on our way even though an Esau with a band of desperadoes should block up the road.

Those forces of God, too, were all engaged personally to attend upon Jacob. I like to set forth that thought: "Jacob went on his way, and the angels of God *met him*"; he did not chance to fall in with them. They did not happen to be on the march and so crossed the patriarch's track; no, no, he went on his way, and the angels of God met him with design and purpose. They came on purpose to meet *him*; they had no other appointment. Squadrons of angels marched to meet that one lone man! He was a saint, but by no means a perfect one; we cannot help seeing many flaws in him, even upon a superficial glance at his life, and yet the angels of God met *him*.

Perhaps in the early morning, as he rose to tend his flocks, he saw the skies peopled with shining ones who quite eclipsed the dawn. The heavens were vivid with descending lusters, and the angels came upon him as a bright cloud descending, as it were, upon the patriarch. They glided downward from those gates of pearl, more famed than the gates of Thebes. They divided to the right and to the left and became two hosts. Perhaps the one band pitched their camp behind, as much as to say, "All is right in the rear, Laban cannot return; better than the cairn of Mizpah is the host of God." Another squadron moved to the front as much as to say, "Peace, patriarch, peace with regard to Esau, the red hunter, and his armed men; we guard you in the van." It must have been a glorious morning for Jacob when he saw not one but many morning stars. If the apparitions were seen in the dead of night, surely Jacob must have thought that day was come before its time. It was as if constellations mustered to the roll call, and clouds of stars came floating down from the upper spheres. All came to wait upon Jacob, on that one man. "The angel of the LORD encampeth round about them that fear him," but in this case it was to one man with his family of children that a host was sent. The man himself, the lone man who abode in covenant with God when all the rest of the world was given up to idols, was favored by this mark of divine favor. The angels of God met *him*. One delights to think that the angels should be willing and even eager, troops of them, to meet one man. How vain is that voluntary humility and worshiping of angels that Paul so strongly condemns. Worshiping them seems far out of the question; the truth lies rather the other way, for they do us suit and service. "Are they not all ministering spirits, sent forth to minister to them that are the heirs of salvation?" They serve God's servants. "Unto which of the angels said He at any time, Thou art my son?" But this He has said, first to the Only Begotten and then to every believer in Christ. We are the sons and daughters of the Lord God Almighty, and these ministering ones have a charge concerning us. As it is written, "they shall bear thee up in their hands, lest thou dash thy foot against a stone."

I have shown you that believers are compassed about with an innumerable company of angels, great in multitude, strong in power, exact in order, punctual in their personal attention to the children of God. Are you not well cared for, oh, you sons of the Most High!

Those forces, though in themselves invisible to the natural senses, are manifest to faith at certain times. There are times when the child of God is able to cry like Jacob, "The angels of God have met me." *When do such seasons occur?* Our Mahanaims occur at much the same time as that in which Jacob beheld this great sight. Jacob was entering upon a more separated life. He was leaving Laban and the school of all those tricks of bargaining and bartering that belong to the ungodly world. He had breathed too long an unhealthy atmosphere. He was degenerating, and the heir of the promises was becoming a man of the world. He was entangled with earthly things. His marriages held him fast, and every year he seemed to get more and more rooted to Laban's land. It was time he was transplanted to better soil. Now he is coming right away;

he has taken to tent life. He has come to sojourn in the land of promise as his fathers had done before him. He was not to confess that he was seeking a city and meant to be a pilgrim until he found it. By a desperate stroke he cut himself clear of entanglements, but he must have felt lonely and as one cast adrift. He missed all the associations of the old house of Mesopotamia, which, despite its annoyances, was his home.

The angels come to congratulate him. Their presence said, "You are come to this land to be a stranger and sojourner with God, as all your fathers were. We have, some of us, talked with Abraham, again and again, and we are now coming to smile on you. You recollect how we bade you good-bye that night when you had a stone for your pillow at Bethel; now you have come back to the reserved inheritance over which we are set as guardians, and we have come to salute you. Take up the nonconforming life without fear, for we are with you. Welcome! welcome! we are glad to receive you under our special care." Then was it true to Jacob, "Verily I say unto you, There is no man that hath left house, or brethren, or sisters, or father, or mother, or wife, or children, or lands, for my sake, . . . but he shall receive an hundredfold now in this time, houses, and brethren, and sisters, and mothers, and children, and lands, with persecutions; and in the world to come eternal life." This brotherhood of angels must have been an admirable compensation for the loss of the fatherhood of that churlish Laban. Anything we lose when we leave the world and what is called "society" is abundantly made up when we can say, We have come unto the church of the first-born, whose names are written in heaven, and unto an innumerable company of angels.

Another reason why the angels met Jacob at that time was, doubtless, because he was surrounded with great cares. He had a large family of little children, and great flocks and herds and many servants were with him. He said himself, "With my staff I crossed this Jordan, and now I am become two bands." This was a huge burden of care! It was no light thing for one man to have the management of all that mass of life and to lead it about in wandering style. But see, there are two companies of angels to balance the two companies of feeble ones. If he has two bands to take care of, he shall have two bands to take care of him; if he has double responsibility, he shall have double assistance. So, brothers and sisters, when you are in positions of great responsibility and you feel the weight pressing upon you, have hope in God that you will have double succor, and be sure that you pray that Mahanaim may be repeated in your experience, so that your strength may be equal to your day.

The Lord's host appeared when Jacob felt a great dread. His brother, Esau, was coming to meet him armed to the teeth and, as he feared, thirsty for his blood. In times when our danger is greatest, if we are real believers, we shall be specially under the divine protection, and we shall know that it is so. This shall be our comfort in the hour of distress. What can Esau do with his four hundred men now that the hosts of God have pitched their tents and have assembled in their squadrons to watch between us and the foe? Do you not see the horses of fire and chariots of fire around about the chosen servant of God? Jacob ought to have felt calm and quiet in heart; I suppose he was while he saw his protectors. Alas! as soon as he lost sight of them, poor Jacob was depressed in spirit again about his brother Esau, lest he should slay the mother with the children. Such is the weakness of our hearts! But let us not fall into the grievous sin of unbelief. We are without excuse if we do so. In times of great distress we may expect that the forces of God will become recognizable by our faith, and we shall have a clearer sense of the powers on our side than ever we had before. O Holy Spirit, work in us great clearness of spiritual sight!

And when you and I, like Jacob, shall be near Jordan, when we shall just be passing into the better land, then is the time when we may expect to come to Mahanaim. The angels of God and the God of angels both come to meet the spirits of the blessed in the solemn article of death. Have we not ourselves heard of divine revealing from dying lips? Have we not heard the testimony so often, too, that it could not have been an invention and a deception? Have not many loved ones given us assurance of a glorious revelation that they never saw before? Is there not a giving of new sight when the eyes are closing? Yes, O heir of glory, the shining ones shall come to meet you on the river's brink, and you shall be ushered into the presence of the Eternal by those bright courtiers of heaven, who on either side shall be a company of dear companions when the darkness is passing and the glory is streaming over you. Be of good cheer; if you see not the hosts of God now, you shall see them hereafter, when the Jordan shall be reached and you cross over to the promised land.

Thus I have mentioned the time when these invisible forces become visible to faith, and there is no doubt whatever that *they are sent for a purpose.* Why were they sent to Jacob at this time? Perhaps the purpose was first to revive an ancient memory that had well-nigh slipped from him. I am afraid he had almost forgotten Bethel. Surely it must have brought his vow at Bethel to mind, the vow that he made to the Lord when he saw the ladder and the angels of God ascending and descending upon it. Here they were; they had left heaven and come down that they might hold communion with him. I like the dream at Bethel better than the vision of Mahanaim for this reason, that he saw the covenant God at the top of the ladder; here he only sees the angels. Yet is there a choice pearl in this latter sight, for whereas at Bethel he only saw angels ascending and descending, he here sees them on the earth by his side, ready to protect him from all ill. How sweetly do new mercies refresh the memory of former favors, and how gently does new grace remind us of old promises and debts. Brother, does not your Mahanaim point to some half-forgotten Bethel? Judge for yourself. Should our glorious God give you at this time a clear view of His divine power and of His covenant faithfulness, I pray that the sight may refresh your memory concerning that happy day when first you knew the Lord, when first you gave yourself up to Him, and His grace took possession of your spirit.

Mahanaim was granted to Jacob not only to refresh his memory, but to lift him out of the ordinary low level of his life. Jacob, you know, the father of all the Jews, was great at huckstering; it was the very nature of him to drive bargains. Jacob had all his wits about him and rather more than he should have had, well answering to his name of "supplanter." He would let no one deceive him, and he was ready at all times to take advantage of those with whom he had any dealings. Here the Lord seems to say to him, "O Jacob, My servant, rise out of this miserable way of dealing with Me and be of a princely mind." Such should have been the lesson of this angelic visit, though it was ill learned. Jacob was prepared to send off to Esau and call him "My Lord Esau"; he was ready to cringe and bow and call himself his servant and all that. He went beyond the submissiveness that prudence suggests into the abject subjection that is born of fear.

The vision should have led Jacob to stand upon higher ground. With bands of angels as his bodyguard, he had no need to persist in his timorous, pettifogging policy. He might have walked along with the dignified confidence of his grandsire Abraham. There is something better in this life after all than policy and planning; faith in God is grander far. A coward's scheming ill becomes the favorite of heaven. Why should he fear who is protected beyond all fear? Esau could not stand against him, for Jehovah Sabaoth, the Lord of Hosts, was on his side. O for grace to live according to our true position and character, not as poor dependents upon our own wits or upon the help of man, but as grandly independent of things seen, because our entire reliance is fixed upon the unseen and eternal.

Jacob as a mere keeper of sheep has great cause to fear his warlike brother, but as the chosen of God and possessor of a heavenly guard, he may boldly travel on as if no Esau were in existence. All things are possible with God. Let us, then, play the man. We are not dependent on the things that are seen. Man shall not live by bread alone, but by every word that proceeds out of the mouth of God. Cursed is he that trusts in man. Trust in God with all your heart. He is your infinite aid. Do the right, and give up calculations. Plunge into the sea of faith. Believe as much in the invisible as in the visible, and act upon your faith. This seems to me to be God's object in giving to any of His servants a clearer view of the powers that are engaged on their behalf.

If such a special vision be granted to us, *let us keep it in memory.* Jacob called the name of that place Mahanaim. I wish we had some way in this western world, in these modern times, of naming places and children, too, more sensibly. We must needs either borrow some antiquated title, as if we were too short of sense to make one for ourselves, or else our names are sheer nonsense and mean nothing. Why not choose names that should commemorate our mercies? Might not our houses be far more full of interest if around us we saw memorials of the happy events of our lives? Should we not note down remarkable blessings in our diaries, to hand down to our children? Should we not tell our sons and daughters, "There God helped your father, boy"; "Thus and thus the Lord comforted your mother, girl"; "There God was very gracious to our family"? Keep records of your race! Preserve the household memoranda! I think it is a great help for a man to know what God did for his father and his grandfather, for he hopes that their God will be his God also. Jacob took care to make notes, for he again and again named places by the facts that there were seen. Jacob named Bethel and Galeed and Peniel and Mahanaim and other places, for he was a great name giver. Nor were his names forgotten, for hundreds of years after, good King David came to the same spot as Jacob and found it still known as Mahanaim, and there the servants of God of another kind met him also.

God's Visible Agents

This brings me to my second text. Angels did not meet David, but living creatures of another nature met him, who answered the purpose of David quite as well as angels would have done. So just for a few minutes we will dwell upon that second event which distinguished Mahanaim. Turn to Samuel 17:27. David came to Mahanaim and there was met by many friends. He stood upon the sacred spot, accompanied by his handful of faithful friends, fugitives like himself. There was not an angel about that day apparently, yet secretly there were thousands flying around the sorrowing king. Who is this that comes? It is not an angel, but old Barzillai. Who is this? It is Machir of Lodebar. They bring with them honey, corn, butter, sheep, great basins by way of baths, and cooking utensils, and earthen vessels to hold their food; look, there are beds too, for the poor king has not a couch to lie upon. These are not angels, but they are doing what angels could not have done, for Gabriel himself could hardly have brought a bed or a basin.

Who is yonder prominent friend? He speaks like a foreigner. He is an Ammonite. What is his name? Shobi, the son of Nahash, of Rabbah, of the children of Ammon. I have heard of those people; they were enemies were they not—cruel enemies to Israel? That man Nahash, you recollect his name; this is one of his sons. Yes! God can turn enemies into friends when his servants require succor. Those that belong to a race that is opposed to Israel can, if God will it, turn to be their helpers. The Lord found an advocate for His Son Jesus in Pilate's house—the governor's wife suffered many things in a dream because of Him. He can find a friend for His servants in their persecutor's own family, even as He raised up Obadiah to hide the prophets and feed them in a cave—the chamberlain to Ahab himself was the protector of the saints, and with meat from Ahab's table were they fed.

It strikes me that Shobi the Ammonite came to David because he owed his life to him. Rabbah of Ammon had been destroyed, and this man, probably the brother of the king, had been spared; this act of mercy he remembered, and when he found David in trouble, he acted gratefully and came down from his highland home with his men and with his substance. Many a good man has found gracious help in his time of need from those who have received salvation by his means. If we are a blessing to others, they will be a blessing to us. If we have brought any to Christ, and they have found the Savior by our teaching, there is a peculiar tie between us, and they will be our helpers. Shobi of Rabbah of Ammon will be sure to be generous to David, because he will say, "It is by him I live; it is through him that I found salvation from death." If God blesses you in the conversion of any, it may be that He will raise them up in your time of need and send them to help. At any rate, either by friends visible or invisible, He will cause you to dwell in the land, and verily you shall be fed.

Here comes another person we have heard of before, Machir of Lodebar. That is the large farmer who took care of Mephibosheth. He seems to have been a truly loyal man, who stuck to royal families even when their fortunes were adverse. As he had been faithful to the house of Saul, so was he to David. We have among us brethren who are always friends of God's ministers; they love them for their Master's sake and adhere to them when the more fickle spirits rush after newcomers. Happy are we to have many such adherents. They helped the preacher's predecessor; they like to talk of the grand old man who ruled Israel in the olden times, and they are not tired of it, but they are the entertainers of the present leader and are equally hearty in their help. God fetches up these brethren at the moment they are wanted, and they appear with loaded hands.

Here comes Barzillai, an old man of fourscore, and as the historian tells us, "a very great man." His enormous wealth was all at the disposal of David and his followers, and he "provided the king of sustenance while he lay at Mahanaim." This old nobleman was certainly as useful to David as the angels were to Jacob, and he and his coadjutors were truly a part of God's forces. The armies of God are varied; He has not one troop alone, but many. Did not Elisha's servants see the mountain full of horses of fire and chariots of fire? God's hosts are of varied regiments, appearing as horse and foot, cherubim and seraphim, and holy men and holy women. Those who are of the church of God below are as much a part of the host of God as the holiest angels above. Godly women who minister to the Lord do what they can, and angels can do no more.

On this occasion Mahanaim well deserved its name because the help that came to David from these different persons came in a most noble way, as though it came by angels. The helpers of David showed their fidelity to him. He was driven out of his palace and likely to be dethroned, but they stood by him and proved that they meant to stand by him. Their declaration was, in effect, "Thine are we, thou son of Jesse, and all that we have." Now was the time of his need, and now he should see that they were not fine-weather friends, but such as were true in the hour of trial. See their generosity! What a mass of goods they brought to sustain David's troops in the day when they were hungering and thirsting. I need not give you the details; the verses read like a commissariat roll of demands. Every actually necessary form of provision is there. How spontaneous was the gift! David did not demand; they brought before he asked. He had not to send round his sergeants to levy upon the outlying villages and farms, but there were the good people ready-handed with all manner of stores. Their thoughtfulness was great too, for they seem to have thought of everything that was wanted, and besides they said, "The people are hungry, and weary, and thirsty, in the wilderness." The heartiness of it all is most delightful. They brought their contributions cheerfully and joyfully, else they would have brought after a meager sort and with less variety of gifts.

I infer from this that if at any time a servant of God is marching onward in his Master's work and he needs assistance of any sort, he need not trouble about it but rest in the Lord, for succor and help will surely come, if not from the angels above, yet from the church below. Will you look at Solomon's Song 6:13, "Return, return, O Shulamite; return, return, that we may look upon thee. What will ye see in the Shulamite? As it were the company of two armies," or *Mahanaim*—for that is literally how it stands in the Hebrew. In the church of God, then, we see the company of Mahanaim; the saints are the angels of God on earth as the angels are His hosts above. God will send those upon His errands to comfort and sustain His servants in their times of need. Go on, O

David, at the bidding of your Lord, for His chosen servants here below will count it their delight to be your allies, and you shall say of them "this is God's host!"

The Host Is the Host of God

And now, to close. While I have shown you God's invisible agents and God's visible agents, I want to call to your mind that in either case, and in both cases, the host is the host of God. That is to say, the true strength and safety of the believer is his God. We do not trust in the help of angels; we do not trust in the church of God nor in ten thousand churches of God put together, if there were such, but in God Himself alone. Oh, it is grand to hang on the bare arm of God, for there hang all the worlds. The eternal arm is never weary, nor shall those who rest on it be confounded. "Trust ye in the LORD forever: for in the LORD JEHOVAH there is everlasting strength." I said last Thursday night to you that faith was nothing but sanctified common sense, and I am sure it is so. It is the most commonsense thing in the world to trust to the trustworthy, the most reasonable thing in the world to take into your calculations the greatest power in the world—and that is God—and to place your confidence in that greatest power. Yes, more, since that greatest power comprehends all the other powers—for there is no power in angels or in men except what God gives them—it is wise to place all our reliance upon God alone.

The presence of God with believers is more certain and constant than the presence of angels or holy men. God has said it, "Certainly I will be with thee." He has said again, "I will never leave thee, nor forsake thee." When you are engaged in Christ's service, you have a special promise to back you up, "Go ye into all the world, and preach the gospel to every creature; and, lo, I am with you alway, even unto the end of the world." What are you afraid of then? Be gone all trembling. Let feeble hearts be strong. What can stagger us? *God is with us.* Was there ever a grander battle cry than ours—the Lord of Hosts is with us? Blessed was John Wesley to live by faith and then to die saying, "The best of all is, God is with us." Shrink? Turn your backs in the day of battle? Shame upon you! You cannot, if God be with you; for "if God be for us, who can be against us?" or if they be against us, who can stand for an hour?

If, then, God is pleased to grant us help by secondary causes, as we know He does—for to many of us He sends many and many a friend to help in His good work—then we must take care to see God in these friends and helpers. When you have no helpers, see all helpers in God; when you have many helpers, then you must see God in all your helpers. Herein is wisdom. When you have nothing but God, see all in

God; when you have everything, then see God in everything. Under all conditions stay your heart only on the Lord. May the Spirit of God teach us all how to do this. This tendency to idolatry of ours, how strong it is. If a man bows down to worship a piece of wood or stone, we call him an idolater, and so he is, but if you and I trust in our fellow-men instead of God, it is idolatry. If we give to them the confidence that belongs to God, we worship them instead of God. Remember how Paul said he did not consult with flesh and blood; alas, too many of us are caught in that snare. We consult far more with flesh and blood than with the Lord. The worst person I ever consult with at all is a person who is always too near me. The Lord deliver me from that evil man—myself. The presence of the Lord Jesus is the star of our night and the sun of our day, the cure of care, the strength of service, and the solace of sorrow. Heaven on earth is for Christ to be with us, and heaven above is to be with Christ.

I can ask nothing better for you, brethren, than that God may be with you in a very conspicuous and manifest manner all through this day and right onward until days shall end in the eternal day. I do not ask that you may see angels; still, if it can be, so be it. But what is it, after all, to see an angel? Is not the fact of God's presence better than the sight of the best of His creatures? Perhaps the Lord favored Jacob with the sight of angels because he was such a poor, weak creature as to his faith; perhaps if he had been perfect in his faith, he would not have needed to see angels. He would have said, "I need no vision of heavenly spirits, for I see their Lord." What are angels? They are only God's pages to run upon His errands; to see their Lord is far better. The angels of God are not to be compared with the God of angels. If my confidence is in Him that He is my Father and that Jesus Christ has become the brother of my soul and that the Holy Spirit dwells in me according to His own word, what need I care, although no vision of the supernatural should ever gladden my eyes? Blessed are they that have not seen and yet have believed. "We walk by faith, not by sight," and in that joyous faith we rest, expecting that in time and to eternity the power of God will be with us, either visibly or invisibly, by men or by angels. His arm shall be lifted up for us, and His right arm shall defend us.

My heart is glad, for I too have had my Mahanaim, and in this my hour of need for the work of the Lord to which He has called me, I see the windows of heaven opened above me, and I see troops of friends around me. For the orphanage now to be commenced I see providence moving. Two camps are around me also, and therefore do I preach to you this day of that which I have seen and known. May the angel of the covenant be ever with you. Amen.

6

An Antidote to Satan's Devices

Now the serpent was more subtle than any beast of the field which the LORD God had made (Genesis 3:1).

Of course, we understand that Genesis 3:1 refers to "that old serpent, called the Devil, and Satan." The Samaritan Version reads, instead of the word *serpent*, "deceiver," or "liar." If this is not the genuine reading, it nevertheless certainly declares a truth. That old deceiver, of whom our Lord Jesus said to the Jews, "When he speaketh a lie, he speaketh of his own: for he is a liar, and the father of it," was "more subtle than any beast of the field which the LORD God had made." God has been pleased to give to many beasts subtlety—to some, subtlety and cunning combined with strength—in order that they may be the more destructive to certain classes of animals whose numbers require to be kept under. To others, that are devoid of very much strength, He has been pleased to give instincts of most marvelous wisdom for self-preservation and the destruction of their prey and for the procuring of their food; but all the wise instincts and all the subtlety of the beasts of the field are far excelled by the subtlety of Satan. In fact, to go further, man has, perhaps, far more cunning than any mere creature, although animal instinct seems sometimes as if it did outride human reason; but Satan has more of cunning within him than any other creature that the Lord God has made, man included.

Satan has abundant craft and is able to overcome us for several reasons. I think it would be a sufficient reason that Satan should be cunning because he is *malicious*, for malice is of all things the most productive of cunning. When a man is determined on revenge, it is

This sermon was taken from *The Metropolitan Tabernacle Pulpit* and was preached on a Thursday evening during the winter of 1858.

strange how cunning he is to find out opportunities to vent his spite. Let a man have enmity against another and let that enmity thoroughly possess his soul and pour venom, as it were, into his very blood, and he will become exceedingly crafty in the means he uses to annoy and injure his adversary. Now, nobody can be more full of malice against man than Satan is, as he proves every day, and that malice sharpens his inherent wisdom so that he becomes exceedingly subtle.

Besides, Satan is *an angel*, though a fallen one. We doubt not, from certain hints in Scripture, that he occupied a very high place in the hierarchy of angels before he fell, and we know that those mighty beings are endowed with vast intellectual powers, far surpassing any that has ever been given to beings of human mold. Therefore, we must not expect that a man, unaided from above, should ever be a match for an angel, especially an angel whose native intellect has been sharpened by a most spiteful malice against us.

Again, Satan may well be cunning now—I may truthfully say, more cunning than he was in the days of Adam—for *he has had long dealings with the human race*. This was his first occasion of dealing with mankind when he tempted Eve, but he was even then "more subtle than any beast of the field which the LORD God had made." Since then, he has exercised all his diabolical thought and mighty powers to annoy and ruin men. There is not a saint whom he has not beset and not a sinner whom he has not misled. Together with his troops of evil spirits, he has been continually exercising a terrible control over the sons of men; he is therefore well-skilled in all the arts of temptation. No anatomist so well understood the human body as Satan does the human soul. He has not been tempted in all points, but he has tempted others in all points. He has tried to assail our manhood from the crown of our heads to the sole of our feet, and he has explored every outwork of our natures and even the most secret caverns of our souls. He has climbed into the citadel of our hearts, and he has lived there; he has searched its inmost recesses and dived into its profoundest depths. I suppose there is nothing of human nature that Satan cannot unravel; though, doubtless, he is the biggest fool that ever has existed, as time continually proves, yet, beyond all doubt, he is the craftiest of fools and, I may add, that is no great paradox, for craft is always folly, and craftiness is but another shape of departure from wisdom.

And now, brethren, I shall for a few minutes first occupy your time by noticing *the craft and subtlety of Satan* and the modes in which he attacks our souls; secondly, I shall give you a few words of admonition with regard to *the wisdom that we must exercise against him* and the only means that we can use effectually to prevent his subtlety from being the instrument of our destruction.

The Craft and Subtlety of Satan

I may begin by observing that Satan discovers his craft and subtlety by *the modes of his attack*. There is a man who is calm and quiet and at ease. Satan does not attack that man with unbelief or distrustfulness. He attacks him in a more vulnerable point than that—self-love, self-confidence, worldliness—these will be the weapons that Satan will use against him. There is another person who is noted for lowliness of spirits and want of mental vigor. It is not probable that Satan will endeavor to puff him up with pride, but examining him and discovering where his weak point is, he will tempt him to doubt his calling and will endeavor to drive him to despair. There is another man of strong, robust bodily health, having all his mental powers in full and vigorous exercise, enjoying the promises and delighting in the ways of God. Possibly Satan will not attack him with unbelief, because he feels that he has armor for that particular point, but he will attack him with pride or with some temptation to lust. He will most thoroughly and carefully examine us, and if he shall find us to be, like Achilles, vulnerable nowhere else but in our heels, then he will shoot his arrows at our heels.

I believe that Satan has not often attacked a man in a place where he saw him to be strong, but he generally looks well for the weak point, the besetting sin. "There," says he, "there will I strike the blow," and God help us in the hour of battle and in the time of conflict! We have need to say, "God help us!" for, indeed, unless the Lord should help us, this crafty foe might easily find enough joints in our armor, and soon might he send the deadly arrow into our souls, so that we should fall down wounded before him. And yet I have noticed, strangely enough, that Satan does sometimes tempt men with the very thing that you might suppose would never come upon them. What do you imagine was John Knox's last temptation upon his dying bed? Perhaps there never was a man who more fully understood the great doctrine that "by grace are ye saved" than John Knox did. He thundered it out from the pulpit, and, if you had questioned him upon the subject, he would have declared it to you boldly and bravely, denying with all his might the popish doctrine of salvation through human merit. But, will you believe it, that old enemy of souls attacked John Knox with self-righteousness when he lay dying? He came to him and said, "How bravely you have served your Master, John! You have never quailed before the face of man; you have faced kings and princes, and yet you have never trembled; such a man as you are may walk into the kingdom of heaven on your own footing and wear your own garment at the wedding of the Most High." Sharp and terrible was the struggle that John Knox had with the enemy of souls over that temptation.

I can give you a similar instance from my own experience. I thought within myself that, of all the beings in the world, I was the most free from care. It had never exercised my thoughts a moment, I do think, to care for temporals. I had always had all I had needed, and I seemed to have been removed beyond the reach of anxiety about such matters. Yet, strange to say, but a little while ago a most frightful temptation overtook me, casting me into worldliness of care and thought. Though I lay and groaned in agony and wrestled with all my might against the temptation, it was long before I could overcome these distrustful thoughts with regard to God's providence, when, I must confess, there was not the slightest reason, as far as I could see, why such thoughts should break in upon me. For that reason and for many more, I hate the Devil worse and worse every day, and I have vowed, if it be possible, by preaching the Word of God to seek to shake the very pillars of his kingdom. I think all God's servants will feel that their enmity against the archenemy of souls increases every day because of the malevolent and strange attacks that he is continually making upon us.

The modes of Satan's attack, then, as you will speedily learn if you have not already done so, betray his subtlety. Ah! sons of men, while you are putting on your helmets, he is seeking to thrust his fiery sword into your heart; while you are looking well to your breastplate, he is lifting up his battle-ax to split your skull; while you are seeing to both helmet and breastplate, he is seeking to trip up your foot. He is always watching to see where you are not looking; he is always on the alert when you are slumbering. Take heed to yourselves, therefore; "put on the whole armor of God"; "be sober, be vigilant; because your adversary the devil, as a roaring lion, walketh about, seeking whom he may devour: whom resist steadfast in the faith"; God help you to prevail over him!

A second thing in which Satan betrays his cunning is *the weapons that he will often use against us*. Sometimes he will attack the child of God with the remembrance of a ribald song or a licentious speech that he may have heard in the days of his carnal state, but far more frequently he will attack him with texts of Scripture. It is strange that it should be so, but it often is the case that when he shoots his arrow against a Christian, he wings it with God's own Word. That seemed to be, according to the poet, the very poignancy of grief, that the eagle, when the arrow was drinking up his heart's blood, saw that the feather that winged it to his bosom had been plucked from his own breast. The Christian will often have a somewhat similar experience. "Ah!" he will say, "here is a text that I love, taken from the Book that I prize, yet it is turned against me. A weapon out of God's own armory is made to be the instrument of death against my soul." Have you not found it so, dear Christian friends? Have you not proved that as Satan attacked Christ with an "It is written," so also has he attacked you? And have you not learned to be upon your guard against perversions of Sacred Scripture and twistings of God's Word lest they should lead you to destruction?

At other times Satan will use the weapon of our own experience. "Ah!" the Devil will say, "on such-and-such a day, you sinned in such-and-such a way; how can you be a child of God?" At another time, he will say, "You are self-righteous, therefore you cannot be an heir of heaven." Then, again, he will begin to rake up all the old stories that we have long forgotten of all our past unbeliefs, our past wanderings, and so forth, and throw these in our teeth. He will say, "What! *you*, YOU a Christian? A pretty Christian you must be!" Or possibly he will begin to tempt you after some such sort as this: "The other day, you would not do such-and-such a thing in business; how much you lost by it! So-and-so is a Christian; he did it. Your neighbor over the road, is he not a deacon of a church, and did not he do it? Why may not you do the same? You would get on a great deal better if you would do it. So-and-so does it, and he gets on and is just as much respected as you are; then why should not you act in the same way?" Thus, the Devil will attack you with weapons taken from your own experience or from the church of which you are a member.

Ah! be careful, for Satan knows how to choose his weapons. He is not coming out against you, if you are great giants, with a sling and a stone; he comes armed to the teeth to cut you down. If he knows that you are so guarded by a coat of mail that the edge of his sword shall be turned by your armor, then will he attack you with deadly poison. If he knows that you cannot be destroyed by that means, seeing that you have an antidote at hand, then will he seek to take you in a trap. If you are wary so that you cannot be overtaken thus, then will he send fiery troubles upon you or a crushing avalanche of woe, so that he may subdue you. The weapons of his warfare, always evil and often spiritual and unseen, are mighty against such weak creatures as we.

Again, the craftiness of the Devil is discovered in another thing—*in the agents he employs.* The Devil does not do all his dirty work himself; he often employs others to do it for him. When Samson had to be over-come and his Nazarite locks to be shorn away, Satan had a Delilah ready to tempt and lead him astray. He knew what was in Samson's heart and where was his weakest place, and therefore he tempted him by means of the woman whom he loved. An old divine says, "There's many a man that has had his head broken by his own rib," and certainly that is true. Satan has sometimes set a man's own wife to cast him down to destruction, or he has used some dear friend as the instrument to work his ruin. You remember how David lamented over this evil, "For it was not an enemy that reproached me; then I could have borne

it: neither was it he that hated me that did magnify himself against me;
then I would have hid myself from him: but it was thou, a man mine
equal, my guide, and mine acquaintance. We took sweet counsel together, and walked unto the house of God in company." "Ah!" says the
Devil, "you did not think I was going to set an enemy to speak evil of
you, did you? Why, that would not hurt you. I know better than that
how to choose my agents. I shall choose a man who is a friend or an acquaintance; he will come close to you and then stab you under the folds
of your garments." If a minister is to be annoyed, Satan will choose a
deacon to annoy him. He knows that he will not care so much about an
attack from any other member of the church; so some deacon will lift
up himself and domineer over him, so that he shall have sleepless
nights and anxious days. If it is a deacon that Satan wants to annoy, he
will seek to set some member or brother deacon against him, and if
there is no other person that he cares for, it shall be his nearest and
dearest friend who shall do the dastardly deed.

The Devil is always ready to take in his hand the net into which the
fish is most likely to go and to spread the snare that is the most likely
to catch the bird. I do not suspect, if you are a professor of long standing, that you will be tempted by a drunken man; no, the Devil will
tempt you by a canting hypocrite. I do not imagine your enemy will
come and attack and slander you; it will be your friend. Satan knows
how to use and to disguise all his agents. "Ah!" he says, "a wolf in
sheep's clothing will be better for me than a wolf that looks like a
wolf, and one in the church will play my game better and accomplish
it more readily than one out of it." The choice of Satan's agents proves
his craft and cleverness. It was a cunning thing that he should choose
the serpent for the purpose of tempting Eve. Very likely Eve was fasci-
nated by the appearance of the serpent. She probably admired its
glossy hue, and we are led to believe that it was a far more noble creature then than it is now. Perhaps, then, it could erect itself upon its
coils, and she was very likely pleased and delighted with it. It may
have been the familiar creature with which she played—I doubt not it
was—before the Devil entered into it. You know how, often, the Devil
enters into each one of us. I know he has entered into me, many a time,
when he has wanted a sharp word to be said against somebody.
"Nobody can hurt that man or grieve that man," says the Devil, "so
well as Mr. Spurgeon can; why, he loves him as his own soul. That's
the man," says the Devil, "to give the unkindest cut of all, and he shall
give it." Then I am led, perhaps, to believe some wrong thing against
some precious child of God and afterward to speak of it. Then I grieve
to think that I should have been so foolish as to lend my heart and
tongue to the Devil. I can therefore warn each of you, and especially

myself and all those who have much love bestowed upon them, to take heed lest they become instruments of Satan in grieving the hearts of God's people and casting down those who have trouble enough to cast them down without having any from us.

And once again, Satan shows his cunning by *the times in which he attacks us*. I thought when I lay sick that if I could but get up from my bed again and be made strong, I would give the Devil a most terrible thrashing because of the way he set upon me when I was sick. Coward! why did he not wait until I was well? But I always find that if my spirit is sick and I am in a low condition of heart, Satan specially chooses that time to attack me with unbelief. Let him come upon us when the promise of God is fresh in our memory and when we are enjoying a time of sweet outpouring of heart in prayer before God, and he will see how we will fight against him then. But, no; he knows that then we should have the strength to resist him, and, prevailing with God, we should be able to prevail over the Devil also. He will therefore come upon us when there is a cloud between ourselves and our God, when the body is depressed and the spirits are weak, then will he tempt us and try to lead us to distrust God. At another time he will tempt us to pride. Why does he not tempt us to pride when we are sick and when we are depressed in spirit? "No," he says, "I cannot manage it then." He chooses the time when a man is well, when he is in full enjoyment of the promises and enabled to serve his God with delight, and then he will tempt him to pride. It is the timing of his attacks, the right ordering of his assaults, that makes Satan ten times more terrible an enemy than he would otherwise be, and that proves the depth of his craftiness. Verily, the old serpent is more subtle than any beast of the field that the Lord God has made.

There is one thing about the powers of hell that has always amazed me. The church of Christ is always quarreling, but did you ever hear that the Devil and his confederates quarrel? There is a vast host of those fallen spirits, but how marvelously unanimous they ever are! They are so united that if at any special moment the great black prince of hell wishes to concentrate all the masses of his army at one particular point, it is done to the tick of the clock, and the temptation comes with its fullest force just when he sees it to be the most likely that he will prevail. Ah, if we had such unanimity as that in the church of God, if we all moved at the guidance of the finger of Christ, if all the church could at this time, for instance, move in one great mass to the attack of a certain evil now that the time has come for the attack upon it, how much more easily might we prevail! But, alas! Satan exceeds us in subtlety, and the powers of hell far exceed us in unanimity. This, however, is a great point in Satan's subtlety, that he chooses always the times of his attacks so wisely.

And yet once more, and I will have done with this point. Satan's subtlety in another thing is very great, that is, *in his withdrawings.* When I first joined the Christian church, I never could make out a saying which I heard from an old man that there was no temptation so bad as not being tempted, nor did I understand then what Rutherford meant when he said he liked a roaring Devil a great deal better than a sleeping Devil. I understand it now, and you who are God's children and who have been for some years in his ways understand it also.

> More the treacherous calm I dread
> Than tempests rolling o'er my head.

There is such a state of heart as this: you want to feel, but you do not feel. If you could but doubt, you would think it a very great attainment; yes, and even if you could know the blackness of despair, you would rather feel that than be as you are. "There!" you say, "I have no doubts about my eternal condition; somehow, I think I can say, though I could not exactly speak with assurance for I fear it would be presumption, yet I do trust I can say that I am an heir of heaven. Yet that does not give me any joy. I can go about God's work; I do feel that I love it, yet I cannot feel it is God's work. I seem to have got into a round of duty, until I go on, on, on, like a blind horse that goes because it must go. I read the promise, but I see no particular sweetness in it; in fact, it does not seem as if I wanted any promise. And even threatenings do not frighten me; there is no terror in them to me. I hear God's Word; I am perhaps stirred by what the minister says, but I do not feel impressed by his earnestness as I should be. I feel that I could not live without prayer, and yet there is no unction in my soul. I dare not sin; I trust my life is outwardly blameless; still, what I have to mourn over is a leaden heart, a want of susceptibility to spiritual delight or spiritual song, a dead calm in soul like that dreadful calm of which Coleridge's ancient Mariner speaks—

> The very deep did rot,
> Alas, that ever this should be!
> Yea, slimy things did crawl with legs
> Upon the slimy sea.

Now, dear friend, do you know anything about your own state of heart just now? If so, that is the answer to the enigma that not being tempted is worse than being tempted. Really, there have been times in the past experience of my own soul when I would have been obliged to the Devil if he had come and stirred me up; I should have felt that God had employed him against his wish to do me lasting good, to wake me up to conflict. If the Devil would but go into the Enchanted Ground and attack the pilgrims there, what a fine thing it would be for them! But, you will notice, John Bunyan did not put him there for there was no business for him there. It was in the Valley of Humiliation that there was plenty of work cut out for Satan, but in the Enchanted Ground the pilgrims were all slumbering, like men asleep on the top of the mast. They were drunken with wine so that they could do nothing, and therefore the Devil knew he was not needed there; he just left them to sleep on. Madame Bubble and drowsiness would do all his work. But it was into the Valley of Humiliation that he went, and there he had his stern struggle with poor Christian. Brethren, if you are passing through the land that is enchanted with drowsiness, indifference, and slumber, you will understand the craftiness of the Devil in sometimes keeping out of the way.

The Wisdom That Overcomes Satan

You and I feel that we must enter the kingdom of heaven, and we cannot enter it while we stand still. The City of Destruction is behind us, and Death is pursuing us. We must press toward heaven, but, in the way there stands this roaring lion, seeking whom he may devour. What shall we do? He has great subtlety; how shall we overcome him? Shall we seek to be as subtle as he is? Ah! that would be an idle task; indeed, it would be a sinful one. To seek to be crafty like the Devil would be as wicked as it would be futile. What shall we do then? Shall we attack him with wisdom? Alas! our wisdom is but folly. "Vain man would be wise," but at his very best estate he is but "like a wild ass's colt." What, then, shall we do?

The only way to repel Satan's subtlety is *by acquiring true wisdom.* Again I repeat it, man has none of that in himself. What then? Herein is true wisdom. If you would successfully wrestle with Satan, make the Holy Scriptures your daily resort. Out of this sacred magazine continually draw your armor and your ammunition. Lay hold upon the glorious doctrines of God's Word; make them your daily meat and drink. So shall you be strong to resist the Devil, and you shall be joyful in discovering that he will flee from you. "Wherewithal shall a young man cleanse his way," and how shall a Christian guard himself against the enemy? "By taking heed thereto according to thy word." Let us fight Satan always with an "It is written," for no weapon will ever tell upon the archenemy so well as Holy Scripture will. Attempt to fight Satan with the wooden sword of reason and he will easily overcome you, but use this Jerusalem blade of God's Word, by which he has been wounded many a time, and you will speedily overcome him.

But, above all, if we would successfully resist Satan, we must look not merely to revealed wisdom, but to *Incarnate Wisdom.* O beloved, here must be the chief place of resort for every tempted soul! We must flee to Him "who of God is made unto us wisdom, and righteousness, and sanctification, and redemption." He must teach us, He must guide us, He must be our all-in-all. We must keep close to Him in communion. The sheep are never so safe from the wolf as when they are near the shepherd. You shall never be so secure from the arrows of Satan as when you have your head lying on the Savior's bosom. Believer, walk according to His example, live daily in His fellowship, trust always in His blood, and in this way shall you be more than a conqueror even over the subtlety and craft of Satan himself. It must be a joy to the Christian to know that in the long run the craft of Satan shall all be disappointed, and all his evil designs against the saints shall prove of no effect.

Are you not looking forward, dearly beloved, to the day when all your temptations shall be over and when you shall land in heaven? And will you not then look down upon this archfiend with holy laughter and derision? I do believe that the saints, when they think of the attacks of Satan, shall "rejoice with joy unspeakable," and besides that, shall feel a contempt in their own souls for all the craft of hell when they see how it has been disappointed. What has the Devil been doing these thousands of years! Has he not been the unwilling servant of God and of His church? He has always been seeking to destroy the living tree, but when he has been trying to root it up, it has only been like a gardener digging with his spade and loosening the earth to help the roots to spread themselves the more. When he has been with his ax seeking to lop the Lord's trees and to mar their beauty, what has he been, after all, but a pruning knife in the hand of God to take away the branches that do not bear any fruit and to purge those that do bear some, that they may bring forth more fruit?

Once upon a time, you know, the church of Christ was like a little brook—just a tiny streamlet—and it was flowing along in a little narrow dell. Just a few saints were gathered together at Jerusalem, and the Devil thought to himself, "Now I'll get a great stone and stop this brook from running." So he goes and gets this great stone, and he dashes it down into the middle of the brook, thinking, of course, he should stop it from running any longer. But instead of doing so, he scattered the drops all over the world, and each drop became the mother of a fresh fountain. You know what that stone was: it was persecutions, and the saints were scattered by it, and then, "they that were scattered abroad went everywhere preaching the word," and so the church was multiplied, and the Devil was defeated. Satan, I tell you to your face, you are the greatest fool that ever breathed, and I will prove it to you in the day when you and I shall stand as enemies—sworn enemies, as we are this day at the great bar of God; so, Christian, may you say to him whenever he attacks you. Fear him not, but resist him steadfast in the faith, and you shall prevail.

7

Another and a Nobler Exhibition

To the intent that now unto the principalities and powers in heavenly places might be known by the church the manifold wisdom of God (Ephesians 3:10).

All the world has been talking during the last three days of the splendid pageant that adorned the opening of the International Exhibition. Crowds have congregated in the palace of universal arts; representatives of all the nations of the earth have journeyed for many a league to view its wonders. Eminent personages of all empires have appeared in the gorgeous spectacle, and such a scene has glittered before the eyes of all men as has never before in all respects been equaled and may not for many a year find a successor to rival it. Wherefore all these gatherings? Why muster, all you nations? Wherefore come you hither, you gazing sons of men? Surely your answer must be that you have come together that you may see *the manifold wisdom of* MAN. As they walk along the aisles of the great Exhibition, what see they but the skill of man, first in this department and then in the other—at one moment in the magnificent, at the next in the minute—at one instant in a work of elegance in ornament, in the next in a work of skill and usefulness. "Manifold wisdom," the works and productions of many minds, the different hues and colors of thought, embodied in the various machines and statues, and so forth, which human skill has been able to produce. We grant you that God has been most rightly recognized there, both in the solemn prayer of the archbishop and in the hymn of the laureate, but still the great object, after all, was to behold the manifold wisdom of man; had

This sermon was taken from *The Metropolitan Tabernacle Pulpit* and was preached on Sunday morning, May 4, 1862.

they taken away man's skill and man's art, what would there have been left?

Brethren, may the greatest results follow from this gathering! We must not expect that it, or anything else short of the Gospel, will ever bring about the universal reign of peace. We must never look to art and science to accomplish that triumph that is reserved for the second advent of the Lord Jesus Christ. Yet may it spread the feelings of benevolence—may it bind together the scattered children of Adam—may it fuse into a happy and blessed union the kindreds of men that were scattered abroad at Babel, and may it prepare the way and open the gates, that the Gospel may proceed to the uttermost ends of the earth!

It is, however, very far from my mind to direct your attention to the marvels that crowd the area of the huge temple of 1862. I invite you, rather, to follow me to a nobler exhibition than this, where crowds are gathering—not of mortals, but of immortal spirits. The temple is not of art and science, but of grace and goodness, built with living stones, cemented with the fair colors of atoning blood, "built upon the foundation of the apostles and prophets, Jesus Christ himself being the chief corner stone"—that temple, the church of the living God, "the pillar and ground of the truth." Into this great palace crowd ten thousand times ten thousand of the host of God, "cherubim and seraphim," or by whatsoever other names those bright intelligences may be known among themselves—"principalities and powers," the different degrees in the hierarchy of immortal spirits, if such there be—they are all represented as intently gazing upon the wondrous fabric that God has reared. Along the aisles of that church, along the ages of its dispensations, stand the various trophies of divine grace and love—the jewel cases of virtues and graces that adorn the believer, the mementos of triumphs gotten over sin and hardness of heart and of victories achieved over temptation and trial; as the spirits walk along these corridors full of divine workmanship, they stand, they gaze, they admire and wonder and speed back their way to heaven and sing more loudly than before, hallelujah to the God whose manifold wisdom they have beheld in the church of God below.

Beloved friends, our text is a strange one. If you will reflect that the angels, the elder-born of creatures when compared with us, have been with God for many an age, and yet I do not know that it is ever said that by anything else they ever learned "the manifold wisdom of God." They were with Him when He made the earth and the heavens. Perhaps during those long periods when the earth was forming—"In the beginning," when "God created the heavens and the earth," the angels were wont to visit this world and to behold alive and in their glory those strange shapes of mystery that now we dig up in fossils from the earth.

Certainly in that day when the earth was without form and void, and
darkness was upon the face thereof, the angels knew the hidden treasure. When He said, "Let there be light: and there was light," when that
first ray of light seemed like a living finger to touch the earth and
waken it to beauty, then seraphic fingers swept their heavenly harps,
and "the morning stars sang together, and all the sons of God shouted
for joy." Yet I do not learn, though they were with the great worker during the seven days of creation, though they saw the cattle after their
kind and the fowls of the air after their kind, and the fish of the sea, and
all the plants and herbs, yet I see not that in all this there was made
known to them the manifold wisdom of God. No more when man, the
Master's last work walked through Eden—when, with his fair consort
by his side, he stood up to praise his Maker, though he was "fearfully
and wonderfully made," though in his mind and body there was a display of wisdom unrivaled before—yet I do not learn that even in man,
as a creature, there was made known the manifold wisdom of God. Yes,
and more than this, when other worlds were made, when the stars were
kindled like glowing flames by light of Deity, if there be other peoples
and other kindreds and other tribes in those myriads of far-off lands, I
do not find in the creation of all those hosts of worlds that bested the
wide fields of ether, that there was then made known to celestial spirits
the manifold wisdom of God. No, more, in all the dispensations of divine providence apart from the church, in all the mystic revolutions of
those wondrous wheels that are full of eyes, apart from the church,
there has not been made known to these beings to the fullest extent the
wisdom of God. Ah! and, brethren, remember yet once more that they
with undimmed eye look upon the glory of Him that sits upon the
throne, so far as it can be seen by created vision. They behold the beatific vision; they are glistening in the splendors of Deity and veil their
faces when at His footstool they cry, Holy, holy, holy, Lord God of
Sabaoth." Yet, though standing as it were in the sun, though they are
foremost of all the creatures, nearest to the eternal throne, I do not read
that by all this they have in the highest sense learned the manifold
wisdom of God.

What an idea, then, does this give us of the importance of the
church! Brethren, never let us despise any more the meanest member of
it, since there is more to be beheld in the church than in creation in its
utmost breadth; more of the wisdom of God in the saving of souls than
in the building the arches of the sky; no, more of God to be seen than
even heaven with all its splendors can otherwise reveal. Oh! let us open
our eyes that we lose not those divine mysteries that angels desire to
look into!

I have now already explained the meaning of the text. We have, therefore, but to direct your attention to *those points of interest upon which angelic intelligence would be sure to linger*. We shall pray that, while we mention these in brief and running catalog, our hearts may be led to meditate much upon the manifold, the varied wisdom of God displayed in the church which Christ has bought with His blood.

The Scheme and Plan of Saving the Church

And first, dear brethren, we think that the grand object of attention in the church to the principalities and powers is the scheme and plan of saving the church. It is this that they so much admire and wonder at. It has been exceedingly well said by others that if a parliament had been held of all the spirits in heaven and in earth and if it had been committed to this general assembly to ordain and fix upon a plan whereby God might be just and yet the justifier of the ungodly, they must all have failed to achieve the task. Those lofty minds, doubtless, consider with delight the fact that in God's way of saving His church, all His attributes shine out with undiminished luster. God is just; they know it in heaven, for they saw Lucifer fall like lightning when God cast him out of his dwelling place on account of sin. God is just, and as much so upon Calvary, where His Son hangs and bleeds "the just for the unjust, to bring us to God," as He was when He cast down the son of the morning. The angels see in salvation this great wonder of justice and peace embracing each other—God as sternly just as if there were not a particle of mercy in His being, smiting His Son for the sin of His people with all the force of His might—God, yet as merciful as if He were not just, embracing His people as though they had never sinned and loving them with a love that could not have been greater had they never transgressed. They understand how God so hated sin that He laid vengeance on His only begotten, and yet "God so loved the world, that he gave his only begotten Son, that whosoever believeth in him should not perish, but have everlasting life." As in the crowns of oriental princes the most precious jewels shone in clusters, so as in one wonderful corona all the infinite attributes of God shine out at once in all their combined glory around Your cross, O Jesu, earth's wonder and heaven's prodigy! This difficulty, so delightfully met, so completely disposed of by the atonement of Christ, causes the angels to behold the manifold wisdom of God.

But, further, when the angels see that by this great plan all the ruin that sin brought upon mankind is removed, they again wonder at the wisdom of God. When they especially notice the way in which it was removed, the strange and mysterious methods that God used for rolling away the stone from the door of the human sepulcher, they yet more bow down with awe. Did we lose Eden in Adam? Lo, the Lord Jesus

Christ has given us a better than Paradise! Did we lose the dignity of manhood? Lo, today we regain it in Christ, for "thou hast put all things under his feet." Did we lose spotless purity? Again we have obtained it in Christ, for we are justified through His righteousness and washed in His blood. Did we lose communion with God? We have obtained it this day, for "we have access by faith into this grace wherein we stand." Did we lose heaven itself? Ah! heaven is ours again, for in Him we have obtained an inheritance and are "made . . . meet to be partakers of the inheritance of the saints in light." And all this mischief is made to destroy itself, God overruling it to be its own destruction: the dragon stung with his own sting; Goliath killed with his own sword; death is slain by the death of the Man who was crucified; sin is put away by the great sin offering, who "bare our sins in his own body on the tree"; the grave is plagued by its own victim since Christ lay a captive within it. Satan casteth out Satan in this case. We rise by man as by man we fell. "As in Adam all die, even so in Christ shall all be made alive." The worm in whom Satan triumphed is the worm in whom God is glorified. It was man whom Satan sought to make the instrument of divine dishonor, and it is man in whom God triumphs over all the crafts and cruelties of hell. This the angels wonder at, for they see in this scheme of salvation, meeting as it does every mischief and meeting it on its own ground, the manifold wisdom of God.

Observe, also, that through the great scheme of salvation by the Atonement, God is more glorified than He would have been if there had been no fall and consequently no room for a redemption. The angels admire the manifold wisdom of God in the whole story of the human race, seeing that in the whole of it, from the beginning to the end, God is more glorified than He would have been had it all been written in letters of gold without one sin or one suffering on the part of the human race. O Lord! when You permitted for a moment Your people to go astray like lost sheep, there might have been silence in heaven, since Your enemy had triumphed, since the precious ones whom You had loved were given up into the hand of the Enemy. When the jewels of Christ were lost for a little season amidst the miry clay and ruins of the Fall, there might have been a furling of Jehovah's banner, for perhaps it seemed to angels as though God had been defeated in His highest praise. But when Christ comes back "from Edom, with dyed garments from Bozrah," wearing upon His royal head the crown in which every jewel is securely set that once was in the hand of the Enemy—when the shepherd comes back from the mountains, bearing on His shoulders the sheep that had gone astray, there is more joy in heaven over the lost ones that are found than there could have been over all of them had they never gone astray. The deep bass of the Fall shall swell the song of the restoration; the hollow moans, as they seemed to be when heard alone, shall but make a part of the grand swell of the eternal song as it shall peal up to the throne of the Lord God of Hosts.

Brethren, if you would think for awhile upon the whole work of God, taking in it the Fall as being foreseen and foreknown, until the day when all the chosen seed shall meet around the throne, I think you will be struck with its glory as a whole. It was within the compass of the power of God to make creatures that would love Him, to make beings that would be attached to Him by the very closest ties. But—I speak with reverence—I do not see how omnipotence itself, apart from the Fall, and the redemption by the sacrifice of Christ when He gave Himself to die for us, could have made such creatures as the redeemed will be in heaven. Brethren, if we had never fallen and never been redeemed, we could never have sung of redeeming grace and dying love. We could not, and the angels could not; we could not have known the heights and depths and lengths and breadths of the love of Christ which passes knowledge. Feasted with heavenly food, we might have admired His bounty, but not as we now do when we eat the flesh of Christ; made to drink the wine pressed from heaven's own clusters, we might have blessed the giver of the feast, but not as we now can do when we drink the blood of Jesus as our sweet wine. Pure and holy, we could have praised Him, and we should have done so, but not as we now can, when we have washed our robes and made them white in the blood of the Lamb.

There is a nearer relationship now than there could have been in any other way, if God had not taken humanity into alliance with Himself, if the Word had not been made flesh and dwelt among us. I say there may have been other plans, but certainly no mortal mind can conceive any other. This seems to be the most wonderful, the most godlike, the most divine, that a creature shall be made perfectly free—that that creature shall offend, shall discover the justice of God through the punishment being laid upon a substitute, but shall learn the love of God through that substitute being God Himself. This creature was ordained to be attached to the Eternal One by ties of filial relationship, by bonds of affection so strong that the pains of the rack and the flames of the fire shall not be able to separate it from the love of God; in heaven this creature shall feel that it owes nothing to itself, nothing to its own natural efforts, but all to Him who loved it and who bought it with His blood, and therefore this grateful being shall praise God after a sort superior by many high degrees to the attainment of any other.

Oh! dear friends, I think if we study the subject for a few hours alone, we shall see that in nothing that God has done is there such a discovery of His wisdom as in the plan of redeeming love. Go round about her, O angels of the Lord; mark well her bulwarks, and tell the towers thereof; consider her palaces; behold the impregnable strength of covenant engagements; see the largeness and broadness of electing love; behold the veracity and truthfulness of divine promises; see the fullness of grace and efficacy in the pardoning blood; see the faithfulness and the immovability of the divine affection when once it is set on men; when you have admired the whole, go back, spirits, and more sweetly than before unite with us in our song—Worthy is the Lamb that was slain to receive honor, and blessing, and majesty, and power, and dominion for ever and ever.

The Dispensations through Which the Church Has Passed

Secondly, without a doubt the wisdom of God is made known to angels and principalities in the various dispensations through which the church has passed. At first the church was indeed a little flock, a few chosen out of the mass—Abram, the Syrian, ready to perish, and a few godly ones in his household. Then the stream widened a little, there became twelve tribes; soon the dispensation became more clear: Moses was raised up, and Aaron, whom God had chosen. Then the angels desired to look into the typical rites and ceremonies of that ancient dispensation. They were pictured standing on the mercy seat with wings outstretched, with their faces bent downward as if they would fain behold the secret that the golden lid concealed. Doubtless, as they saw the sacrifice, whether it was the burnt offering, the peace offering, or the sin offering—as they saw the gorgeous ceremonies of the tabernacle or the yet more splendid rites of the temple—they admired the wisdom of God as it was set forth in the dim symbol and shadow. How much more must they have admired it when the Sun of righteousness arose with healing beneath His wings, when they saw the sacrifice superseded by the one great offering, the high priest set aside by the Man, who having once offered one sacrifice forever, sat down at the right hand of the Majesty on high; how they have marveled since that time as truth after truth has been expounded in the experience of believers, as doctrine after doctrine has been revealed to the church of Christ by the illuminations of the Holy Spirit! Oh! brethren, the angels, when they compare the past with the present and again, the present with the past, the choosing of the Jewish olive and the leaving out of the rest of the trees and anon, the grafting in of the Gentiles from the wild olive and the casting out of the natural branches, how they must have admired the singular variety of God's dispensations, when they know, as certainly they do, that His grace remains the same!

In climbing or in descending a lofty mountain, one is struck with the sudden change of views. You looked on the right just now, and you saw a populous city on the plain; you turn a corner and looking through a break in the forest you see a broad lake; in a moment or two your road winds again, and you will see a narrow valley and another range of mountains beyond. Every time you turn, there is a new scene presented to you. So it would seem to the angelic spirits. When first they began to ascend the hill on which the church stands, "Jerusalem which is above, . . . the mother of us all," they saw the wisdom of God manifested as Abraham saw it; a turn in the road, and they saw it as Moses beheld it; another, and they had a view as David was wont to gaze upon it; anon, when they ascended to clearer light and the mists that hung about the mountainside had all been scattered and had fallen in one gracious shower of grace, they saw it as the apostles beheld it when they stood upon Mount Olivet; and since then, through every trial of the church, as the eighteen centuries have rolled on since the Master went up to heaven, they have been constantly catching fresh views and seeing fresh manifestations of the varied and constantly changing wisdom of the un-changing God as it is manifested in His dealings to the church. So that both in the dispensations, as well as in the man, there is made known to principalities and powers the manifold wisdom of God.

The Church's Covenant Head and Representative

Thirdly, to be brief upon each point, we may conclude without any doubt that they mainly see the wisdom of God in His church in the church's covenant head and representative. Oh! when first they heard that the Lord of life and glory was to be made flesh and to dwell among men, how they must have admired the plan of heaven's going down to earth that earth might come up to heaven! The Babe in the manger commanded all their songs. When they saw that Babe become a Man and heard Him preach, how they must have marveled at the wisdom of sending God Himself to be God's own prophet! When they saw that Man living a life of perfect holiness, how they must have clapped their wings at the thought that man could see perfection now in God's own self shrouded in human form! But when it came to atonement and they learned that God's people must be crucified in Christ, how struck must they have been as the thought burst upon them for the first time, that the whole host of the elect were to sweat great drops of blood through one Man—that they were to be flagellated, to be scourged, bruised, and spat upon, in one Man—that the host of the chosen were to carry the cross of their condemnation upon one Man's shoulders—that that one Man was for them all to take all their load of guilt and, nailed to the tree, bleed away His life for the whole body. Oh! I say, when they saw that lowly Man, with all the sins of the whole chosen company resting upon His shoulders, and knew this soli-tary Man to be God—able to carry the whole—they must have marveled, indeed, at the wisdom of God. And when that triumphant Man cried, "It is finished!" having drained the cup of damnation to its utmost dregs, until there remained not one man descended into the grave, and the whole company of the faithful were buried with Him, oh, how they marveled! When again they beheld the second Adam bursting His cerements, rending the chains of death as though like another Samson He had broken the chains of the Philistines as though they were but string, how astonished they were when they thought that the elect were risen in that glorified person! And when that Man was received up into heaven and the cloud hid Him from mortal view, how they rejoiced to see Him rise! but much more to think that we also were risen in Him and in Him had ascended up on high—in Him the whole church, I say, leading their captivity captive! When that representative personage, with acclamation beyond all measure, rose to the throne of the Father and took His seat at the right hand of the dreadful Majesty on high, how wonderful must have been the admiration of the spirits when they thought that He had raised *us* up together and made *us* sit together in heavenly places in Christ Jesus! Perhaps there is no doctrine that is more astounding to Christians than this. I know if we want a theme that will enlarge our minds, the subject of the union of the chosen with Christ is certainly the most expansive.

> O sacred union, firm and strong,
> > How great the grace, how sweet the song,
> That worms of earth should ever be
> > One with incarnate Deity!
>
> One when he died, one when he rose,
> > One when he triumphed o'er his foes;
> One when in heaven he took his seat,
> > And angels sang all hell's defeat.
>
> This sacred tie forbids all fears,
> > For all he has and is is ours;
> With him our head we stand or fall,
> > Our life, our surety, and our all.

The manifold wisdom of God, in thus constituting Christ the covenant head and representative of the elect in all its various shapes and shades, must have been discovered to angelic beings. Though that were a theme that might require a full discourse, we leave it at once to turn to another.

The Conversion of Every Child of God

In the fourth place, the manifold wisdom of God is made known to principalities and powers in the conversion of every child of God.

There are some very singular implements in this present great Exhibition, marvelous feats of human skill, but there is one thing they have not there that is to be found in the church of the living God, and that is a heart melter, an instrument for turning stone to flesh. There are inventions for melting granite and for liquefying flints, but I know of no invention but one, and that is not to be found in any earthly show, for melting the adamant of the human heart. Now when the Lord takes the profane man or the infidel or the proud, self-righteous Pharisee or some tall, hectoring, careless sinner and casts his heart into a fountain filled with Jesus' blood and it begins to melt with penitence, the angels see the matchless wisdom of God. And I am sure, also, that there is not in the Exhibition another instrument called a heart healer, an invention for binding up broken hearts and making them one again and healing all their wounds, but the Lord is pleased by the same instrument by which He breaks hearts to heal them. That blood that melts the flint restores us the heart of flesh. Having first melted the heart, He next shows His matchless skill by taking away despair, despondency, and terror, and giving to the poor conscience perfect peace and rest, no, exulting joy and boundless liberty. As the angels see the proud man bow his knee, as they hear him in his silent chamber pour out his heart in sighs and groans, they say, "It is well, great God; it is well." As they see him come down from that chamber light of foot and joyous of heart because his sin is all forgiven, with his groans all turned into songs, the angels say, "It is well, great God; it is well; Thou woundest, but Thou dost heal; Thou killest, and Thou makest alive."

Conversion is the greatest prodigy that we know of. If there are no such things as miracles today, believe me I have neither eyes nor ears. But you say, "What miracles?" I answer, not miracles in smitten rocks that yield rivers of water or seas that are divided by prophetic rod, but miracles in hearts and consciences obedient to holy, heavenly power. I have seen in my short life more miracles and stranger than Moses ever ought and wonders great as Christ Jesus Himself ever performed on flesh and blood, for they are His miracles today that are wrought through the Gospel. If it were well just now, I might point to some in these galleries and on this ground floor and ask them to tell what miracles God did for them and how they are here in one happy circle today for the praise of God, men who once were everything that was vile, but they are washed, but they are sanctified. The tears start in their eyes now when they think of the drunkard's cup and of the swearer's oath with which they were once so well acquainted, ah! too, and of the dens and kens of filth and of lasciviousness which they once knew, and they are here, loving and praising their Lord. Oh! there are some in this house today who, if they could speak, would say they are the greatest sinners out of hell and the mightiest wonders out of heaven. If our Gospel is hid, it is only hid to those who willfully shut their eyes to it.

When one sees harlots reclaimed, and thieves, drunkards, swearers made to be saints of the living God, do not tell us that the Gospel has lost its power. O sirs! do not dream that we shall believe you while we can see this power, while we can feel it in our own souls, while every day we hear of conversions, while scarce a week rolls on without some score of brands being plucked from the eternal burning. And, I say, if the church of God on earth admires these conversions, what must angels do who are more acquainted with the guilt of sin and know more of the loveliness of holiness and understand better the secret heart of man than we do? How must they gladly and exultingly admire in each distinct conversion, as it presents phases different from any other, the manifold wisdom of God! That ingenious toy called the kaleidoscope at every turn presents some new form of beauty, so the different converts who are brought to Christ by the preaching of the Word are every one unlike the other, there is something to distinguish each case, hence by them to the very letter our text is proved, the manifold wisdom, the much varied wisdom of God is displayed. I have sometimes understood the word *manifold* as comparing grace to a precious treasure that is wrapped up in many folds, first this, then the next, then the next must be unfolded, and as you unwrap fold after fold, you find something precious each time; but it will be long before you and I shall have unwrapped the last fold and shall have found the wisdom of God in its pure glittering luster, lying stored within as the angels behold it in the church of the living God.

The Trials and Experience of Believers

But time has failed me, and therefore I must leave points upon which I wanted to dwell. The principalities and powers to this day find great opportunities for studying the wisdom of God in the trials and experience of believers, in the wisdom that subjects them to trial, in the grace that sustains them in it, in the power that brings them out of it, in the wisdom that overrules the trial for their good, in the grace that makes the trial fit the back or strengthens the back for the burden. They see wisdom in the prosperity of Christians when their feet stand like hinds' feet upon their high places; they see the same in the despondencies of believers when even in the lowest depths they still say, "Though he slay me, yet will I trust in him." As every day brings to us our daily bread, so every day brings to heaven its daily theme of wonder, and the angels receive fresh stores of knowledge from the ever-new experience of the people of God. They lean from the battlements of heaven today to gaze on you, you tried believers; they look into your furnace as did the king of Babylon, and they see the fourth man with you like to the Son of God. They track you, O children of Israel, in the wilderness; they see the places of your encampment and the land to which you are hastening; as they mark the fiery cloudy pillar that conducts you and the angel of God's house that leads the van and brings up the rear, they discover in every step of the way the wonderful wisdom of God.

The Last of God's People Shall Be Brought In

And lastly, beyond all controversy, when the last of God's people shall be brought in and the bright angels shall begin to wander through the heavenly plains and converse with all the redeemed spirits, they will then see the manifold wisdom of God. Let the angel speak awhile for himself. "Here," says he, "I see men of all nations and kindreds and tongues, from Britain to Japan, from the frozen north to the burning zone beneath the equator; here I see souls of all ages, babes hither snatched from the womb and breast and spirits that once knew palsied age to whom the grasshopper was a burden. Here I see men from all periods, from Adam and Abel down to the men who were alive and remained at the coming of the Son of God from heaven. Here I see them from the days of Abraham and the times of David and the period of the apostles and the seasons of Luther and of Wycliffe, even to the last times of the church. Here I see them of all classes. There is one who was a king and at his side, as his fellow, is another that tugged the oar as a galley slave. There I see a merchant prince who counted not his riches dear to him and by his side a poor man who was rich in faith and heir of the kingdom. There I see the poet who could sing on earth of *Paradise Lost* and *Paradise Regained*, and by his side one who could not put two words together, but who knew the Paradise lost and the Paradise regained within the Eden of his own nature, the garden of his own heart. Here I see Magdalene and Saul of Tarsus, repenting sinners of all shades and saints of all varieties, those who showed their patience on a lingering sick bed, those who triumphed with holy boldness amid the red flames, those who wandered about in sheepskins and goatskins, destitute, afflicted, tormented, of whom the world was not worthy; the monk who shook the world and he who cast salt into the stream of doctrine and made it wholesome and pure; the man who preached to his millions and brought tens of thousands of souls to Christ, and the humble cottager who knew but this Bible true and herself the partaker of the life of Christ—here they all are, and as the spirits wander and look first at this and then at that—first one trophy of grace and then at another monument of mercy, they will all exclaim, "O LORD, how manifold are thy works in wisdom hast thou made them all." Heaven is full of Your goodness which You have wrought for the sons of men.

And now, dear friends, the sermon is done when I ask you just these questions; the first shall be a question for the children of God, and the other for those who know Him not.

First, to the children of God: Do you think you and I have sufficiently considered that we are always looked upon by angels and that they desire to learn by us the wisdom of God? The reason why our sisters appear in the house of God with their heads covered is "because of the angels." The apostle says that a woman is to have a covering upon her head because of the angels, since the angels are present in the assembly and they mark every act of indecorum, and therefore everything is to be conducted with decency and order in the presence of the angelic spirits. Think of that, then, when this afternoon we shall be talking together. Let us not talk in such a way that a visitor from heaven might be grieved with us; when we are in our general assemblies met together, let us not discuss ignoble themes, but let the matters that we discuss be truly edifying, seasoned with salt. Especially in our families, might we not say more about Christ than we do? Do we not often spend days, perhaps weeks, without making any mention of such things as we could wish angels to hear? You are watched, brethren, you are watched by those that love you. The angels love us and bear us up in their hands lest we dash our feet against the stones. They encamp about our habitations; let us entertain these royal guests. Since they cannot eat our bread and sit at our table to partake of our good cheer, let us talk of subjects that will delight them in a manner with which they shall be gratified, and let their presence be to us a motive why we should so conduct ourselves that to angels and principalities may be made known by us the wisdom of God.

And lastly, what, think some of you, would angels say of *your* walk and conversation? Well, I suppose you don't care much about them, and yet you should. For who but angels will be the reapers at the last, and who but they shall be the convoy of our spirits across the last dark stream? Who but they shall carry our spirits, like that of Lazarus, into the Father's bosom? Surely we should not despise them. What has your conduct been? Ah, sirs, it need not that the preacher speak. Let conscience have her perfect work. There are some here over whom angels, could their eyes have known a tear, would have wept day and night. You have been almost persuaded to be Christians. You have known the struggles of conscience, and you have said, "I would to God I were altogether such as the saints are!" but you are unconverted still. Stay, spirit, guardian spirit, you who have watched over this son of a sainted mother, wing not back your disappointed flight to heaven! He relents, he relents. Now the Spirit of God is moving in him. "*It shall be*," says he, "*it shall be*," "I repent and believe in Jesus," but oh, spirit, you will be disappointed yet, for he is about to say, "In a little time, go your way for a little season; when I have a more convenient season I will send for you." Angel, you will be disappointed yet, but if the soul shall say, "Now, even now, in this house of prayer, I cast myself upon the finished atonement of Christ; I trust in Him to save me"; wing your flight aloft, you glorious angel, tell the cherubs around the throne that the prodigal has returned, and an heir of heaven has been born; let heaven keep holiday, and let us go into our homes rejoicing, for he that was dead is alive again, and he that was lost is found.

May the Spirit of God do this, for Jesus' sake! Amen.

8

Angelic Studies

To the intent that now unto the principalities and powers in heavenly
places might be known by the church the manifold wisdom of God
(Ephesians 3:10).

T he "principalities and powers in heavenly places" to whom the
apostle here refers, are, no doubt, the angels. These bright and
glorious spirits, never having fallen into sin, did not need to be
redeemed, and therefore, in the sense of being cleansed from guilt, they
have no share in the atoning sacrifice of Christ. Yet it is interesting to
notice how our Lord did as it were pass and repass their shining ranks
when He sped His way down to the regions of death and when He came
back triumphant to the realms of glory. Thus in one place "we see Jesus
. . . made a little lower than the angels for the suffering of death," and in
another place we learn, that the Father "raised him from the dead, and
set him at his own right hand in the heavenly places, far above all prin-
cipality, and power, and might, and dominion." It is possible that the
mediation of Christ has a bearing upon them and has henceforth confirmed them in their holiness, so that by no means shall they ever be
tempted or led into sin in the future. It may be so, but this much seems
to be evident, that though they had no direct share in redemption, they
feel nevertheless an interest in it and are to be instructed by its results.
The sublime plan of the Gospel of the grace of God, which is so entirely beyond the compass of our natural faculties that we could never
by searching have found it out, appears to have been equally beyond the
grasp of angelic intelligence—a mystery that excited their wistful in-
quiry—until by the church (that is to say, by the divine counsel and
conduct in forming and perfecting the church) there is made known to
them the manifold wisdom of God as they have never learned it before.

This sermon was taken from *The Metropolitan Tabernacle Pulpit* and was
preached on Sunday evening, May 1, 1870.

They have kept their first estate and have been obedient to God's behests. They delight to be known as the servants of God, doing His commandments and hearkening to the voice of His word.

They are appointed to exercise some sort of power over various parts of God's creation, hence they are called "principalities and powers." Certainly they are engaged in hymning Jehovah's praise. Much of the music that rises up before His throne comes from the harps of spirits, pure and immaculate, who have never known sin. Yet, though they are thus pure, thus engaged in worship, of such eminent rank in the universe of God, they are never represented as indifferent spectators of anything that our mortal race can do or suffer, but their sympathy with men is constant. Do they not watch over the saints? Is it not written that they encamp round about them that fear the Lord? Are they not charged to take care of the saints, to bear them up in their hands, lest they dash their feet against the stones?

Angels, we know, have often been messengers of God's will to the sons of men. They have never shown any reluctance; on the contrary, great has been their joy to bear God's tidings down from heaven to earth, and their sympathy even with fallen men, with men who have grievously sinned and gone astray, is shown by the fact that they rejoice over one sinner that repenteth, more than over ninety and nine just persons that need no repentance. They are, as it were, in yonder gilded vessel, untossed of tempest, but they have sympathy with us in this poor, heavy-laden boat, tossed with tempest and not comforted. I see them there on yonder sea of glass mingled with fire. I hear their harpings as incessantly their joy goes up in music to the throne of the Most High. But they do not look down with scorn on us poor denizens of this dusky planet. On the contrary, they delight to think of us as their brethren, as their fellow servants, as it will be the consummation of their happiness when we shall all be gathered to the church of the firstborn, that they shall make up the innumerable company of angels that surround the blood-washed throng.

Angels See the Manifold Wisdom of God through the Church

How exclusively through the church do angels come to see the manifold wisdom of God? Who can doubt that *the angels had seen much of the wisdom of God in creation?* With faculties keener and more elevated than ours, faculties that have never been blunted by sin, they can perceive the various contrivances of God's skill both in the animate and the inanimate world. Doubtless as each new star has been minted by God, as each planet has been struck off like a spark from the everlasting anvil, angels, those sons of the morning, have lifted up their songs and have poured forth their plans of joy and gladness. They have seen the wisdom of God in the greatness of creation; in every sphere they have been able to perceive it, for their vision is far more comprehensive than ours. And they have also, no doubt, seen that wisdom in all its minuteness as manifest in the delicate structure of organized beings and the skillful economy of the operations of creative power, for there again they are able with the singleness and certainty of superior optics to perceive what only after long years we have been able to discover, and that by reasoning from the ingenuity of the works to the excellence of the design.

What a scale of survey must a seraph have! How readily can we imagine an eye that takes in at once the landscape of the world! He need not confine himself to one single spot in God's universe, but with rapid wings he can steer far and wide over the infinity of space. May he not pause here a moment and there a moment and with a glance peer into the multiform wisdom of God in all the ten thousand thousand worlds that stud the realms of space? Yet with all that facility of observation, it seems that the angels have some parts of the wisdom of God to learn and some lessons of heavenly science to study which creation cannot unfold to their view, to be ascertained and certified by them only through the transcendent work of redemption that the Lord has carried on in His church.

Fix your attention for a moment on the word *now* as it is used in the text. On that word, it seems to me, much of the meaning hangs. Long before our Lord came into the world, God had been pleased to reveal somewhat of the wisdom of His grace in the types of the old law. These were full of significance but at the same time not free from perplexity to the minds of most men. They appear not to have been very intelligible even to the angels, for they are pictured as standing over the mercy seat with wings outspread, looking down upon its golden lid, anxiously inquiring, but not clearly discovering, the secret of the old covenant dispensation. Peter says, I suppose in allusion to this, "which things the angels desire to look into." But Paul here vehemently sets forth the yearnings of his heart in the exercise of his ministry, "to make all men see what is the fellowship of the mystery, which from the beginning of the world hath been hid in God, who created all things by Jesus Christ: to the intent that *now* unto the principalities and powers in heavenly places might be known by the church the manifold wisdom of God." May we not infer from this that though angels saw Moses and Aaron and the long succession of priests that followed them, though they doubtless mingled invisibly in the solemn gatherings that went up to Mount Zion and heard the chantings of the glorious psalms, that though they saw the streams of blood that flowed at the altar of burnt offering and marked the rising clouds of smoke that went up from the altar of incense that was in the Holy Place before the Lord, they had not as yet discovered the wisdom of God in its fullness and clearness, the spotless mirror of His power, the reflex image of His glorious perfection, but it must have remained for them to learn it from the church? Since Christ has come, angels are to be students of the manifold wisdom of God as revealed in His work toward His people, preparing them for that grand climax, the espousal of the church and the marriage of the Lamb.

To come closer to the matter we must trace it progressively, as though it were step-by-step that the angels pursued their study and acquired an insight into this manifold wisdom. It may be they do so. Certainly among the children of men there is much pleasure in the getting of knowledge; the merchandise of it is better than the merchandise of silver, and the gain thereof than fine gold. As we gradually break up fresh ground, decipher that which is obscure, sift out analogies, solve difficulties, and follow out the tracks of history in one continuous line, our enjoyment of study rises to enthusiasm. Do you not think that the angels perceived the manifold wisdom of God *now that they began to understand what man was and what man is?* They must have already seen that God had created an order of pure spirits who served Him faithfully and never sinned. There was one form of wisdom displayed in that. Other spirits, equally pure, went astray, and in the wisdom of God, for there is wisdom in it, these were suffered to continue astray, reserved in chains until the judgment.

Anon the angels perceived that God was about to make another intelligent creature, not altogether spiritual, but a spiritual creature that should be linked with materialism, a creature that should abide in a body of clay, and that God intended to make this creature a mixture of earth and heaven—such a one that he should occupy the place that fallen angels had left vacant. They discerned in this at once the wisdom of God. He had formed a pure spirit; He had fashioned material substances; now He was about to make a creature in which the two should be combined, a creature that should be spiritual and yet should be material.

But, before this creature should be permitted to take his place forever at the right hand of God, he was to be permitted to pass the test of temptation; being tempted, he was to fall into sin; out of the condemnation into which he should sink he was to be elevated by an act of grace; from the guilt of that sin he was to be cleansed by a matchless system of substitutionary sacrifice; then, after having been alienated in heart, he should nevertheless become as pure as if he had never been conscious of evil. Contaminated with it he should be redeemed from it and stand in allegiance to the Most High, to serve Him with as absolute a perfection as if he had never transgressed or lost his first estate. Herein is manifold wisdom, that the Lord God should make so strange a creature that he should be formed of the dust of the ground and yet created in the image of God; a creature that should know sin and whatever of pleasure there might be in it, and yet be restored to purity and holiness; a creature who though awhile estranged in heart and guilty of rebelling with a high hand against his Creator, should return to its allegiance through the infinitely wise workings of God's Spirit and henceforth should remain forever the faithful servant of God and, something more, the child of God, lifted up and exalted into a nearness of connection and intimacy of communion with the Great Father of Spirits into which no creature had ever been brought before. In that grand design, the angels must have seen much of the sublime wisdom of God, and that conspicuously through the church.

But, brethren, may not the admiration of angels at the unfolding of this wisdom have been increased by the mystery in which it had long been shrouded from their apprehension? Observe that Paul was exulting in a revelation "which in other ages was not made known unto the sons of men as it is now revealed unto his holy apostles and prophets by the Spirit." What use will he make of it? First he looks around among the saints and sounds the note of welcome; then he looks out among his fellowmen and proclaims it to the Gentile world; at length he looks up and descries among the angelic throng creatures of noble mind and exalted rank, who could sympathize the joy and hail the solution of so grand a problem. Be it remembered that the decree had previously been proclaimed from the throne of the Most High, for, "when he bringeth in the first begotten into the world, he saith, And let all the angels of God worship him"; yet the means by which the counsels of God concerning Christ and the church should be brought to pass had not thus far been shown.

With what pleasing wonderment, therefore, would the principalities and powers in heavenly places regard the plan as it was unsealed! How well might the apostle look forward to those ages to come that have yet to prove the reality of all that has been foreshadowed, the truth of all that has been prophesied, and (the work now in progress being completed) the actual form and fashion of all that from the beginning was predestinated. Even while the mystery was unexplained, it was not for pure angelic minds to doubt; still their thoughts must have been full of marvel, and startling questions must have occurred to them. Shall the only begotten Son of the Father take the nature of man into union with the Godhead? Can it be safe to put such a creature as man into so sublime a relationship with the Creator? Will pride never inflame his breast and provoke his soul to transgress? By what strange process shall he be made to partake of the inheritance of the saints in light? While the details are concealed, the destiny seems incomprehensible. It is therefore that the church becomes as a museum which angels may visit with ever-expanding interest and ever-increasing delight; over the minutest particulars of the divine workmanship in the saints they may pore with pleasure, for there they have open to their observation by the church the manifold wisdom of God. And all this redounds to the glory of the Savior.

That creature, man, when thus elevated, can never be proud, for he remembers what he was. If ever the feeling of exultation crosses his mind, he transfers the honor to Christ, who can receive it as his rightful due. There is not in heaven, of all the creatures, a humbler creature, though none more elevated, made to have dominion over all the works of God's hands, with all things put under his feet, made to be akin to Deity itself by virtue of union with the Son of God and yet safe to stand there without cause to fear that he should pervert his high prerogative or usurp any adoration or prerogative that does not belong to him. The process through which he has passed, his annealing, as it were, in the fire of his fall and of his repentance, his deep obligations to sovereign grace shall make it safe to grant that he shall sit with Christ on His throne, even as Christ also overcame and is set down with His Father on His throne. I talk of these things feebly and superficially, but I am persuaded that this is a subject that angels can think of with enchantment, and as they think it over, they see transparent proofs of the manifold wisdom of God.

But to come down to more familiar topics, probably you will be more impressed with the excellence of this wisdom as you look at the first principles of Christianity than would arrest your attention in any refinements of reasoning. The wisdom of God is clearly seen by angels in this, that though *God was dishonored in this world by sin, that sin has redounded to His greater honor.* Satan, when he led men astray and tempted them to rebel, thought he had marred the glory of God, but he never did more palpably outwit himself. As Augustine ventured to say of the fall, "Happy thought," so, when we see how God's mercy and His love have shone resplendent through that dreadful breach, we can only admire the wisdom of God that has thus outmatched the subtlety of hell. The serpent was exceeding wise, but God was wiser far. Satan's craft was dexterous, but God's wisdom was infinite in its prescience. Wisdom has outmatched craft. Is it not glorious to think that this world where God was dishonored most is the world where He shall be most revered? There is no such display of the attributes and perfections of Godhead in the whole universe beside as there is here. On our blighted soil God has stood foot to foot with moral evil. God incarnate, the Son of God has sustained the conflict and won the victory; for while the heel of Christ was bruised, the head of the dragon has been most effectually broken! A triumph that God would have us commemorate in time and in eternity has come through the sin that threatened the destruction of the world.

This wisdom of God is to be seen *in the way that our redemption was wrought*. The doctrine of substitution is a marvel that, if God had never revealed, none of us could by any possibility have discovered. You remember how it was. We had sinned and were condemned. How could God be gracious and yet be just? How could He keep His law and yet at the same time show His mercy toward us? Of old that problem was solved by the suretyship of Christ. He who had determined to be man put Himself, from before the foundation of the world, into our place and offered Himself to God as the head of the race, in covenant, that He might make recompense to the broken law. Angels could not have conjectured this, but when it was made known to them, how could they refrain to chant fresh songs to the praise of Him who could undertake so loving a responsibility?

It became necessary when Christ was our surety that He should afterward take upon Himself our nature. Oh, how it must have surprised the angels when they heard that the Son of God was coming down to earth to be born of a virgin! What marvel must there have been when the announcement was made through the courts of paradise that He was going down to Bethlehem! One of the angelic number who had been sent to attend Him proclaimed His advent, but while he was making the announcement, "Suddenly there was with the angel a multitude of the heavenly host," who now came in to swell the song, "Glory to God in the highest, on earth peace, good will toward men." The swell of that music, how grand! The cadence of those simple words, how charming! Yes, the angels must have discovered something of the wisdom of God when they saw that God thus tabernacled among men, that the Word was made flesh in order to be capable of carrying out His surety engagements and really become a substitute for those who had offended.

I think His whole life must have struck them with wonder. They must often have observed wisdom in His actions and in His prayers, in His speech and in His silence, but when at last He came to die, I think even cherubim and seraphim were wrapped in amazement. That He should stoop from heaven and become a friend to the fallen race might surprise them much, but that He should stoop to die must have appeared utterly incomprehensible. Something more of the love and wisdom of God should yet be revealed to them. I think our hymn must fitly describes how they gathered around that cross—

> And could their eyes have known a tear,
> They must have wept it there.

When they beheld the griefs and torments of the dying Son of God, the Lamb of God's Passover, when they heard Him say, "It is finished!" what a door must have been opened to them! They saw then that He had finished transgression, made an end of sin, and brought in an everlasting righteousness; then, perhaps, they saw more clearly than before how Christ by suffering put an end to our sufferings and by being made a curse for us had made us the righteousness of God in Him. If they marveled during the three days of His slumber in the tomb, His resurrection must have opened up another door to them. And, when after His forty days' sojourn they came to meet Him with glad acclaim, when they joined Him and with Him rode up to the gates of heaven singing, "Lift up your heads, O ye gates; and be ye lifted up, ye everlasting doors; and the King of glory shall come in," when they came in triumph with the Lord mighty in battle, the King of glory, in that procession to His throne they must still have been more and more amazed and have said one to another, "What thing is this; what mighty marvel! He that became Man to suffer is the very one that now rises to reign; He who was born to die now lives forevermore. Behold, He is now the head over all things and made to have dominion over all the works of God's hands, for it hath pleased the Father that in Him should all fullness dwell!" Thus, brethren, though time and voice fail me, permit me to say the whole history of our blessed Lord, who is the Head of the church, is making known to the principalities and powers in heavenly places the manifold wisdom of God in such a way as they never could have otherwise seen it.

The wisdom of God is seen through the church *in the Holy Spirit's work* as well as in the work of Christ. It is "*manifold* wisdom." You know the children's toy, the kaleidoscope. Every time you turn it there is some fresh form of beauty. You seldom see the same form twice. So it is with nature, each time and season has its special beauty. There is always variety in its scenery; diversities of form and color are strewn throughout the world. You never saw two hills molded to the same pattern or two rivers that wound after the same fashion from their source down to the sea; nature is full of variety. So is the work of the Holy Spirit. In calling sinners to Christ there is singleness of purpose but no uniformity of means. Your conversion, my dear friend, in the main outline is very like mine, yet your conversion has its distinctive incidents. God's wisdom is displayed equally in bringing you in that way and in bringing me in another way. I believe there will be found evidence at the last of the wisdom of God in the very date, the very place, the very means in and by which every soul is brought to believe in Jesus, and angels will, no doubt, be able to perceive in every conversion some singular marks of beautiful originality proceeding from the inexhaustible Artist of Grace, the Holy Spirit. That same wisdom will be seen in the biography of every convert—how the Lord afflicts or how He comforts, how He upholds us, how He keeps back that which cannot yet be endured, how He gently leads us, how He makes us to lie down. We find fault sometimes with the way of Providence because we do not understand it; when we shall get a clearer sight of it, we shall see that every mark and line was dictated by His love and ordered by His infinite counsel. *As each Christian shall be conformed to the likeness of Christ*, angels will see in the products of grace fresh displays of the manifold wisdom of God.

I could suppose that the death of a martyr must be such a spectacle as those holy watchers regard with extraordinary interest. Would they not have gathered around such a woman as Blandina, for instance, who was made to sit in a red-hot chair after having been tossed upon the horns of a wild bull, yet constant to the last she maintained her faith in Christ while passing through the torture? Pure spirits as they were, they must have commiserated the physical anguish and admired the spiritual triumph of this feeble woman thus devoted in her love to their Lord and Master. Yes, you ministering spirits, you who *live* to serve our Eternal King, surely you must rejoice at the loyalty of those servants of His who *die* for His truth. In late years, since this house of prayer was built when the martyrs of Madagascar were burned at their stakes for Christ, as they stood erect in the fire and began to sing, the angels, celestial vocalists as they are, must have been ravished with a music that they could not emulate; when they breathed the prayer, "Into thy hands we commend our spirits," the angels must almost have envied them the ability of serving God in that sphere of suffering and the possibility of bearing in their bodies the marks of the Lord Jesus. Aye, and when they have seen your boldness and your constancy, your self-denial and your patience and heard your importunate prayers and groans as you have pleaded for the souls of others, seeking with tears to bring others to Jesus, I do not doubt that they have ascribed to the manifold wisdom of God the production of such luscious fruits from such inferior creatures—fruits that bring to His name so much of glory and so much of renown to His grace. In all the saints, through the history of their vocation and the development of their sanctification, angels can discern the manifold wisdom of God.

The subject is far too large for me. I shall leave you to think it out after thus introducing you to but a few aspects of it. There is much room for meditation as to how these bright and happy spirits do and shall see the wisdom of God in the salvation of the church.

Angels Gain through the Church

Do angels gain anything by the church of God? I think they do.

Certainly they *acquire increased knowledge.* With us knowledge is sometimes sorrow. To know is often to mourn. What the eye does not see the heart does not rue. Where ignorance is bliss—and it sometimes is—there are those who think 'tis folly to be wise. But ignorance is not bliss in heaven. Knowledge increases the joy of the angels, and I will tell you why—because it makes them take a greater delight in God when they see how wise and gracious He is. If it is possible for the angels to be happier than natural innocence and honorable service can render them, they must be happier through knowing and seeing more of God as His attributes are reflected and His perfections mirrored forth in the church.

Angels, I think, *will be enriched by the society of the saints in heaven.* Commerce always enriches, and commerce between angelic and human natures will be enriching to them both. They love in heaven; they show their love by rejoicing over repenting men. They will be glad to see us there. I do believe they will make much of us, as we do if we have seen some poor child reclaimed and afterward grow up to honor; we like to think of such a one; it brings the tears into our eyes that our father did so good a deed for the orphan, the pauper, or the outcast. And will not the angels rejoice over those in whom the Father's mercy has wrought such wonderful happiness?

Again, to my imagining (can it be illusive?) angels are gainers by the church because they *get nearer to the throne of God than they were before.* Another order of beings, our own, to wit, is advanced. Surely when one creature gets near to God, all unfallen creatures are promoted. God, in vital union with the creature, was not to be conceived of until Christ came down to earth and clothed Himself in manhood, thus raising creatureship nearer to God by just that length; so angels by inference seem to me interested in the honor that Jehovah has put on His works—the endowed works of His own formation.

Do you not think, too, that perhaps they *can see God better in Christ than even they did before?* Is it not possible that even they who veiled their faces with their wings in the presence of the Almighty, because the brightness of glory was excessive, may now stand with unveiled faces and worship God in Christ? I think it is so. They never saw much of God before until they saw God veiled in human flesh. There was too dazzling a splendor for them until the interposing medium of the manhood of Christ came in between them and the absolute Deity. It may be so.

And may not there be *a reflex sense of gratitude* in the very heart of angels when they see us in heaven or while they see us wending our way thither, as they perceive what it would have cost to have restored them had they been beguiled by sin and therefore what debtors they are to God that they were never suffered to fall? Does it not make their state and standing more and more joyful to them when they see in us how the righteous scarcely are saved and at what an expense men were lifted up from the ruins of death and the dread doom of the damned? Why, I think they say not one to another, with Pharisaism: "We thank You, great God, that we are not as men are." No, they say, with lowliness of mind: "We bless You, O God, that we were permitted to stand in our fidelity and were not left to the natural weakness which might have succumbed to temptation, for You charged even Your angels with folly, but You have held us, and here we are to bless Your name." It may be so; it may be so.

Lessons for Us

What is all this to us? *Ought it not to make us prize the Gospel?* If the angels think so much of it, oh! what should we think? If they who have only seen it esteem it so, how ought we to value it who have tasted it? If they admire the veins that filled the fountain, what shall we say who have washed in that fountain? If they wonder at Christ, who took not on Him the nature of angels, how shall we admire Him who espoused the house of Abraham and the seed of Adam? Let us appreciate the Gospel beyond all price, emolument, or honor.

How, too, should we study the Gospel, if it is the research of angelic intellects! Is the church their schoolbook whence they learn lessons of the divine wisdom, because no science is equal to that of the wisdom of God in Christ revealed in His church? O be not, you converts, ignorant of the Word of God; be not oblivious of the operations of God in your own souls! The angels desire to look into these things. Do you look into them? Blessed shall you be if you abide in the study of the Word of God! You shall be like trees planted by the rivers of water, that bring forth their fruit in their season. O do apply every faculty you have to acquire increasing knowledge of that which angels love to study.

And now take courage, you feebleminded ones, and *never fear again the sneer of the man who calls the Gospel folly.* Account him to be the victim of folly who despises this manifold wisdom. Shall I set the judgment of a poor, puny mortal against the judgment of an angel? I suppose that even Newton and Kepler and Locke and those mighty master spirits would be mere infants compared with seraphs. Those great men loved to study the Scriptures, and when your modern pretenders to a little smack of philosophy come in and sneer at our holy Gospel, we can well afford to sneer at them. What are their sneers to us? In proportion to a man's ignorance is generally his impudence when he meddles with the Gospel. I think it was Hume who confessed that he had never read the New Testament and said he never would; yet he was one of the most glib in caviling at that of which he nothing knew. Ah! you skeptics, sciolists, and scoffers, we can well afford to let you rail, but you can ill afford to rail when angels are awed into wonder, and so would you be if there were anything angelic about your temper or anything of right wisdom in your attainments.

Last of all, if this be so, *how we ought to love Christ who have a saving interest in the Gospel, and how they ought to tremble who have it not!* Unsaved men, unsaved women, if it wants manifold wisdom to save men, then men's ruin must be very great, and your peril must be very imminent. If it amazes angels to see how God saves, it must be a terrible destruction from which He saves. That destruction is coming upon you; its dark shadows have already begun to gather around you. How great is your folly to refuse a salvation so wise, to reject a Savior so attractive as Jesus! Think of His loving gentleness, and consider the simple way in which He saves—believe and live. The supplies necessary for your salvation are all waiting. There is nothing to be done; it is all complete. There is nothing to be found; it is all ready. Salvation is finished. What a fool must he be that will not have it! O stretch out your withered hand and take it! God give you power. If you say, "How?" I answer thus: Trust, trust, trust. Come and confide in Christ. Rely upon Christ, and He will save you. God grant you grace to do it at once, and He shall have the praise. Amen.

9

Angelic Protection in Appointed Ways

For he shall give his angels charge over thee, to keep thee in all thy ways (Psalm 91:11).

Our subject this morning was the sprinkling of the blood of the paschal lamb upon the lintel and the two doorposts of the houses of the children of Israel in Egypt. As soon as that was done and the lamb had been eaten, they had to start upon their journey to Canaan. They knew that they had to go, and they were prepared to go. They had their loins girt, and each man had his staff in his hand and his sandals on his feet. After being prisoners so long, they were set free in order that they might become pilgrims to the land that the Lord their God had given to their fathers.

We who have believed in the Lord Jesus Christ are in a similar condition to theirs, for the Lord has redeemed us, and we can sing the new song, "He hath brought us up out of the house of bondage, and with a high hand and an outstretched arm He hath made us free." And now we are pilgrims and strangers in this world, for we are on our way to a better land than the earthly Canaan ever was—a land that flows with something richer than milk and honey and where there is an eternal and abounding portion appointed for each one of the redeemed.

We are pressing on through this great wilderness toward the land into which the Lord will surely bring us in His own good time. Our text is a promise to pilgrims. It most appropriately follows the text of this morning: "The blood shall be to you for a token." You have set out upon the road to heaven; you have entered the narrow way by Christ who is the gate at the head of the way, and now you are wondering how you

---

This sermon was taken from *The Metropolitan Tabernacle Pulpit* and was preached on Sunday evening, August 22, 1875.

will get on while you are on the road and whether you will be preserved in the right way so as to endure to the end. This promise comes to you with much of real heart cheer, "He shall give his angels charge over thee, to keep thee in all thy ways."

Some Ways Are Not Included in This Promise

My first remark is rather by way of implication from the text than in direct exposition of it. It is this, there are some ways that are not included in this promise because they are not our ways and they are not God's ways, but they are ways into which we may be tempted by Satan and which we are jealously to avoid.

You know how, when the Devil professed to quote this text to our Lord, he left out the latter part of it, "to keep thee *in all thy ways*," because it would not have suited his purpose to mention that proviso. We, however, will begin with the words that the Devil omitted, since the very fact of his omission of them seems to show how essential they are to a right understanding of the meaning of the text. O Christian, if you keep to the King's highway, you will be safe, but there are byways and, alas! crooked lanes down which you must not go; if you do go there, you will go at your own hazard. He who travels on the King's highway is under the King's protection; he who takes to byroads must protect himself, and the probability is that he will meet with robbers who will make him rue the day that ever he turned to the right hand or to the left.

So, first, we must take care that we never go in *the ways of presumption*. This is what Satan would have had Christ do. "Cast thyself down," said he, "for it is written, He shall give his angels charge over thee, to keep thee." This temptation to presumption is by no means an uncommon one. I have heard of it from the lips of men who were evidently not the children of God, or they would have resisted the temptation and not have yielded to it as they did. They have said, "Well, we are God's children, so we may do as we like. We are saved, therefore we may live as we please"—a dreadful inference from what, to other men, might be a precious truth. O dear friends, beware of tempting the Devil to tempt you! Beware, too, of tempting the Lord your God, as some do who venture a long way into evil company or into doubtful paths under the mistaken notion that they are so prudent that they will not be overtaken as others might be—that they are so sage, and withal so experienced, that they may go where young people must not venture and may do a great many things that less-instructed Christians had better not touch. Where you think you are perfectly safe, there you are often most in danger. Horses frequently fall just at the bottom of the hill, when the driver thinks that it is unnecessary to rein them up any longer. When you are so foolish as to say, "Now I am out of the reach of temptation," you are in the very midst of temptation; when you think you are not being tempted at all, you are being tempted the most by the very fancy that you are not being tempted.

O beloved friends, beware of presuming! Some have been so favored in the dispensations of providence, so prosperous in everything they have undertaken, that they have thought they might speculate as far as ever they pleased, and at last—well, they have had very shady characters at the end of their lives. They have done once what they never ought to have done; because it succeeded, they have been tempted to do it again and yet again. But, I pray you, sirs, never gather from the success of a wrong action that God is willing for you to repeat it; rather say, "God was very gracious to me in not punishing me that time, but I will never run such a risk as that again." I do not believe that Jonah, after having been once thrown into the sea and cast forth upon the shore by the whale, ever wanted to be flung into the sea again; he might not have felt certain about another whale coming along to carry him to land. If you have been miraculously delivered once from the great deep, do not put yourself into such a position again. If you do, you may find that the next great fish is a shark, not a whale, and instead of being brought to land, you may be destroyed. In brief, beware of all presumptuous ways, for God has not promised to keep you there

And, brethren, you scarcely need to be told that you cannot expect to be preserved if you go into *sinful ways*. I trust that you do watch against the more coarse and vulgar sins to which others are prone and that you will not be allowed to fall into them, but there is such a thing as falling by little and little. Mind, I pray you, the little evils. A man never falls into the great, unclean sins of lust all at once; it is usually by a long series of little familiarities that he reaches that terrible end. He is indecorous first, indecent next, and then, at last, criminal. Oh, keep back, keep back from the beginnings of evil. If you keep back at the very first, you will go no further, but if you slide just a little, you will find that this world is such a slippery place that you will surely fall, and fall frightfully, too. I trust that no Christian man would practice dishonesty in his business, yet you know that it is very easy for one to do a wrong thing because it is "the custom of the trade." "They label this 100 yards, though it is only 90, but if I label it 90, I shall not sell it, and in the next shop it will probably be marked 110, so I must label mine a little more than it is." Well, if you do, recollect that you are a thief. Though it is the custom of the trade, you are a liar if you conform to it, and you cannot expect God's blessing upon you in doing it. Do you think that in the Day of Judgment God will say to men, "You are not guilty, for that deception was the custom of the trade"? By no means; what does the Lord care about the customs of your trade? Do right, at all hazards; if you do wrong, you do it at your peril, for you have no promise from God that He will keep you in such a way as that. I need not enlarge upon this point, because you know as much about such things as I do; and, therefore, you can make the application to your own particular case. But, O Christian, do keep altogether clear of every evil way! May God's grace preserve you from straying into Bypath Meadow!

The man who professes to be a Christian must not expect God's angels to keep him if he goes in *the way of worldliness*. There are hundreds, and I fear thousands, of church members who say that they are the people of God, yet they appear to live entirely to the world. Their great aim is moneymaking and personal aggrandizement, just as much as it is the aim of altogether ungodly men. The kingdom of Christ, the needs of His church, the wants of perishing souls have a very slender place in their hearts; they live wholly for themselves, only they try to conceal it under the plea of providing for their families. "Seek ye first the kingdom of God, and his righteousness; and all these things shall be added unto you," is a text from which we need to preach to professing Christians throughout London and throughout the whole world.

There is also *the way of pride* which many tread. They must be "respectable"; they must move in "Society"—with a big S, and everything is ordered with a view to display. To be great, to be famous, to be esteemed, to keep up a high repute—it is for this that they live. And some grow very strong, in a Christian sort of way, in that line; they profess to have attained to a "higher life" than ordinary Christians ever reach. I am not at all anxious to get up there, for I do not believe there is any higher life in this world than the life of God that is given to everyone who believes on the Lord Jesus Christ. The highest life I aspire to is to live as Jesus Christ lived and to walk as He walked, and that is the lowest kind of life with which any Christian ought to be contented. When we get such fine feathers as these, they do not make us fine birds.

There is also *the way of willfulness* which I have known some follow. Very grievous is it to see some, whom we really think to be good men, shift their quarters apparently without any reason. They were doing very well, yet away they rush, for they cannot let well alone. Some brethren seem to be afflicted with a kind of perpetual fidgetiness. They are rolling stones and gather no moss. They move from one position to another, not because there is any need for them to move, but just because they cannot stay still. They go away from their nest and away from their home and very often act in direst opposition to the order of God's providence. Oh, beware of that spirit of willfulness! We may get to be so very strong in the head that we may have to suffer there. It is often wise, as the old saying puts it, to take advice of our pillow. He who does not sleep upon a thing may have to weep upon it. Better look before you leap. Always follow the cloud of God's providence, don't run before it; for, if you run before it, you may find it hard work to get back again. Many have acted thus to their cost and of course have had no blessing resting upon them in doing so.

One other way in which a Christian ought not to go is *the way of erroneous doctrine.* I know some professors who, as soon as a new heresy comes up, want to have taste of it. I confess that I never felt much temptation in that direction. I do not suppose, if you went into a chemist's shop, you would say to him, "I have heard of somebody being killed at Norwood by taking such-and-such a poison; I should like a taste of it." You would not ask him to take down his big bottles and to give you a taste of all the deadly poisons he had in stock. "Oh, no!" you say, "we are in our right senses; we should not do such a foolish thing as that." Yet I know people who, as soon as ever there is any teaching spoken of as being erroneous, say, "We must have a look at that; we must have a taste of that"—never satisfied except when they are tasting poisons.

There is a period in life when a Christian should obey Paul's injunction to the Thessalonians, "Prove all things," but let him get that done as quickly as he can, and then let him get to the second part of the injunction, "Hold fast that which is good." Never hold anything fast until you have proved it to be good, but do not be everlastingly proving it. Some things do not need any proving; they bear upon their forefront their character. But others need to be proved; so, having proved the right things to be right and the true things to be true, hold them fast, and turn not aside from them. About every six weeks there is a new doctrine promulgated; sometimes, there is a new sect started. It is simply because there is somebody away there, up in his study, who is sorely troubled with bile or dyspepsia. He never went out to try to win a soul; he never did any practical work for Christ, but he edits a newspaper or he writes for a magazine, and out of that wonderful brain of his, which is full of cobwebs, he excogitates a new doctrine. There are certain people who are always waiting for such novelties, and straightway they run off with it and spread it wherever they can. These false-doctrine-makers and their disciples are the curse of the age in which we live. I implore you, my friends, to abide in the good old paths. What you know to be true, that hold fast. Your father's God and your mother's God forsake not; as for the truths that God has taught you by His own Spirit, grapple them to you as with hooks of steel, for if you go in the way of error, you cannot expect divine protection.

In Some Ways Safety Is Guaranteed

There are ways in which safety is guaranteed. There is, first, *the way of humble faith in the Lord Jesus Christ*. You know that way, brother, so walk in it. Oh, to be nothing and to let Christ be everything—to confess your own guilt and to be clothed in His righteousness! Keep to that safe road, for it is the King's highway of which it may be said, "No lion shall be there, nor any ravenous beast shall go up thereon, it shall not be found there; but the redeemed shall walk there."

There is, next, *the way of obedience to divine precepts*. Do what God tells you, as God tells you, and because God tells you, and no hurt can come to you. The Lord told Moses to take by the tail the serpent from which he fled; he did so and he was not bitten, but the serpent stiffened into a wonder-working rod. Obey the Lord in all things. Mind the jots and the tittles, for whosoever shall break one of the least of Christ's commandments, "and shall teach men so, he shall be called the least in the kingdom of heaven: but whosoever shall do and teach them, the same shall be called great in the kingdom of heaven." Oh, to follow in the footsteps of the Lord Jesus Christ, step-by-step, and to keep closely to His footprints! It is in such ways that angelic protection will be afforded to us.

There is also *the way of childlike trust in providential guidance*. Happy is that man who always waits upon God to know what he shall do—who asks the Lord ever to guide him and who dares not lean upon his own understanding. Watch the Lord's providential leadings; wait for divine guidance. It is far better to stand still than to run in the wrong road. Pause a while, and pray for direction, and do not move until you hear the voice behind you saying, "This is the way, walk ye in it." In such a road as that, angels will certainly guard you.

There is, too, *the way of strict principle and stern integrity*. Traveling along that road will often involve a good many losses and crosses and much reproach, and sometimes it will even appear to destroy your usefulness. But I charge you—young men especially—never violate any principle that you profess to hold. I believe that it has been a lasting blessing to some, whom I know, that they have scorned to trim their sails, even in the smallest degree, to please any living soul. Do you the same. Be just, and fear not. Keep to a cause that is despised if you believe it is a right one, and love it all the more because it is despised. Ask not what will pay, care not for the flatterer's smile. Pursue truth even though she may go along very rough roads; she will always repay you in the long run. Cling to her and win her smile; then the frowns of the whole world need not cause you a moment's thought. The way of principle is the way of safety; God's angels will keep you if you keep to that road.

And, dear brethren, I am quite sure that *the way of consecrated service for God's glory* is another of these safe ways. It is well when a man says, "I choose my path by this rule—how can I best serve my God? Having judged whether there is any principle involved and having a fair choice between this and that, I say to myself, 'In which way can I hope to be the more useful? In what course of life can I best glorify God?'" That is your way to heaven, Christian—the way in which your Master can get the most glory out of you, and, if you walk in that way, you may depend upon it that you will be protected by His sovereign power.

And once again, there is *the way of separation from the world and close walking with God.* No man ever suffered any real injury through keeping himself aloof from the ways of ungodly men, and, on the other hand, no man ever failed to be a gainer by close and intimate fellowship with God. "Enoch walked with God," and he gained not only escape from the pangs of death but also the testimony that "he pleased God." O Christian men, could not more of us choose this blessed path and walk in it continually? If we did so, we should have the fulfillment, in its deepest meaning, of the promise of our text, "He shall give his angels charge over thee, to keep thee in all thy ways."

Right Ways Will Lead to Differing Circumstances

These right ways will lead us into differing circumstances. Sometimes, *the right way will lead us into very stony places*, positions of great difficulty, yet here is the promise to meet that emergency, "They shall bear thee up in their hands, lest thou dash thy foot against a stone." A way is nonetheless right because it is rough. Indeed, often it is all the more sure to be the right way because it is so displeasing to flesh and blood.

Sometimes, also, *the right way may be very terrible with temptation.* If your path is so beset, do not, therefore, imagine that it is a wrong way because the psalmist goes on to say, "Thou shalt tread upon the lion and adder." Lions and adders will come to you, temptations will threaten to devour you even while you are in the right road, but then you are promised that, as long as it is the right road that you are in, you shall get the victory over the lion and the adder. The temptation may be of so mysterious a character that you cannot understand it. It may be like a dragon, but if so, here is your comfort, "the young lion and the dragon shalt thou trample under feet."

And remember, beloved friends, that even if the road is not stony and if no lion attacks you, you will be kept from *the perils of the smooth and easy roads.* You will always need divine and angelic keeping, for God would not have charged His angels to keep His people in all their ways if they did not need protection in all their ways. Some of you are just now prospering in business, but your way is not any safer than the way of the man who is losing his all; indeed, yours may not be as safe as his. To you who are in robust health, I venture to say that your path is more perilous than the path of the man who is always ailing, and to all of you I say, do pray for angelic keeping. Ask the Lord still to guard you with His celestial hosts, or else in many of your ways, be they rough or smooth, you will fall to your serious hurt.

Right Ways Will Lead to Security

While walking in all right ways, believers are secure. O Christian man, if you have not violated your conscience—if you have not forsaken the path of communion with your God, think what high privileges are yours! First, *God Himself concerns Himself about you.* He charges His angels to take care of you. David, when his soldiers went to battle against his rebellious son Absalom, specially charged their leaders to deal gently with the young man for his sake, but he charged them in vain. In a far higher sense, God charges His angels to guard His saints, and He does not charge them in vain. This is not a more general command; it is a sort of imperative personal charge that God lays upon His angels. "Take care of My children; they are in My road—the King's high road of rectitude. Watch over them, and do not suffer them to be hurt." So you have God personally charging His angels to take care of you.

Next, *you have mysterious agencies to protect you.* "He shall give *his angels* charge over thee." We speak of dragons, but we do not know much about them; we do not know much about angels, but we feel sure that angels can overcome dragons, for they are more than a match for devils. If mysterious temptations come to you, there shall also be mysterious defenders to thrust them back. You have more friends, poor Christian, than you know of. When you are fighting the battles of God, you may hear a rush of angel wings at your side if you only have your ears divinely opened. If all men forsake you, God can send His angels, though you see them not, to strengthen you in some secret manner that I cannot fully explain. "Behold, the mountain was full of horses and chariots of fire round about Elisha," the prophet who dared to be true to his God and to serve Him faithfully. God would sooner empty heaven of all the angelic host, cherubim and seraphim included, than allow any one of His people who has walked in His ways to suffer defeat. He charges all His angels to take care of His saints and to keep them in all right ways.

And *as angels are on our side, so are all things, visible and invisible.* Why believers, the very stones of the field are in league with you, and the beasts of the field are at peace with you. Wherever you go, you have friends ready to help you. It is true that you have enemies among the wicked, but their weapons shall not prevail against you, and wherever there is a messenger of God—be it wind or storm or lightning or hail—it is your friend. The very stars in their courses fight for you. The forces, terrific and tremendous, which at times shake the world, are only your Father's flaming swords unsheathed to protect you. If we are walking in the ways of God, we truthfully sing—

> The God that rules on high,
>   And thunders when he please,
> That rides upon the stormy sky,
>   And manages these:
>
> This awful God is ours,
>   Our Father and our love;
> He shall send down his heavenly powers
>   To carry us above.

Sing then, saints of the Lord, for everything is on your side. "Ye shall go out with joy, and be led forth with peace: the mountains and the hills shall break forth before you into singing, and all the trees of the field shall clap their hands."

What a very sweet thought is suggested by the word "thee" in our text! It teaches us that *each one of the saints is personally protected.* "He shall give his angels charge over *thee,* to keep *thee* in all thy ways." God takes a personal interest in every traveler along the right road and charges His angels to keep him. Perhaps you say, "I do not read the text, sir, as referring to me." Well, I think you should do so. When you read the precept, "Thou shalt not steal," do you suppose that it refers to you? "Oh, yes!" you say, "I would not like to suggest that it did not mean me; I would not plead exemption from the precept." Well, then, my dear brother, do not seek to be exempted from the promise. Just as you feel sure that the precept applies to you, so, as a child of God, feel sure that the promise applies to you. "He shall give his angels charge over *thee*, to keep *thee* in all *thy* ways."

This protection is perpetual, as well as personal; God's angels are "to keep thee *in all thy ways"*—in your ups and your downs, in your advancements and your retirings—when you are asleep and when you are awake—when you are alone and when you are in company—if you have to preach and if you have to hear—if you have to serve and if you have to suffer. You always need keeping, and you shall always have it, for the angels are "to keep thee in all thy ways."

And how beautiful it is to remember that *all this keeping brings honor with it*. "He shall give *His* angels charge over thee." Notice that He shall give *His* angels—the very angels that wait upon God and see His face—the very angels that are the bodyguard of the Eternal—"He shall give *His* angels charge over *thee*." "Mark you," says the Lord to Gabriel or Michael or whatever the angel's name may be, "I charge you to take special care of that poor girl, for she is a daughter of mine. Take care of that poor man whom so many despise, for he is a prince of the blood imperial. He belongs to me; he is an heir of God and joint-heir with Jesus Christ." Oh, what amazing dignity this promise puts upon the very least and lowliest of the followers of the Lamb!

Note just one more point, that *all these privileges come to us by Jesus Christ*, for Christ is that mystic ladder that Jacob saw; up and down whose wondrous rungs the angels came and went. The commerce between the saints and heaven is kept up by way of the person of the Lord Jesus Christ. Oh, what joy is this! If Christ is yours, angels are yours, and all the principalities and powers in the heavenly places will delight to take care of you.

Now, if anyone here is going home to a lonely room, I should like you to feel that you are not going there alone. Father and mother are away in the country, perhaps, and some of you young people feel quite alone in London, but if you are believing in the Lord Jesus Christ, you are not alone, for the Lord of all the holy angels is with you, and an innumerable company of blessed spirits is round about you. Take comfort from this glorious truth. God's mysterious angelic agency, which you see not and hear not, but which is most true and real, will form a cordon round about you to protect you in the midst of the temptations of this great city. If you are but faithful to Him and keep in His ways, nothing shall hurt you between here and heaven. There may be many darts hurled at you, but the great shield of faith shall turn them all aside or quench them forever. You will have to encounter many temptations and trials, but you will be preserved amid them all. I heard a Primitive Methodist minister, speaking last Friday night, make use of a very strong expression while describing what a man could do by faith. He said, "He cannot only overcome a legion of devils, but he could kick his way through a lane of devils if he did but rest in God." I have had that idea in my mind ever since I heard him use that expression, and I am sure that it is true, for some of us have had to do it already. Those devils are great cowards; so when God once takes entire possession of a man, he need not fear even though all hell were let loose upon him. One butcher is not afraid of a thousand sheep, and one man whom God makes strong can put to rout all the hosts of hell, and he need not fear all the trials of life whatever they may be. "If God be for us, who can be against us?"

In closing, there are two or three thoughts that I think are worth remembering. The first is this. Dear brethren, we see from this text that *the lowest employment is consistent with the highest enjoyment.* The angels are our nurses, "they shall bear thee up in their hands," just as nurses hold up little children who are not able to stand by themselves. Those angels continually behold God's face and live in the perfect bliss of heaven, yet they condescend to do such humble deeds as these. Dear brother, be like the angels in this respect; teach an infant class in the Sunday school, yet keep your face bright with the light of God's countenance. Give away tracts, go and visit among the poor, look after fallen women, or do any other work for the Lord that needs to be done. Never mind what it is, but remember that the employment is all the more honorable because it appears to be so commonplace. Never was Christ grander, I think, than when He washed His disciples' feet; certainly, never are we more like Him than when we also are willing to wash their feet or render any lowly service that they may need.

The next thought is *as angels watch over us, how cheerfully ought we to watch over one another!* How gladly you who are older in the divine life ought to watch over the younger ones of the Lord's family! If God enables you to have any of the joy of angels over repenting sinners, mind that you take some of the care that angels exercise over those who walk in God's ways. What can I, the pastor of this huge church, and my brother and all the elders do by way of watching over five thousand of you? You must pastorize yourselves to a large extent. Watch over one another. "Bear ye one another's burdens, and so fulfill the law of Christ." Visit each other in your sicknesses, seek to bring back to Christ and the church all the backsliders whom you can find,labor for the good of one another, for in this way only can our task be done, and you shall be like the angels if you bear up the feeble ones in your hands lest they trip up and fall to their grievous hurt.

Then, next, *how safe and happy we ought to feel when we know that God has charged the angels to take care of us!* Do not be so nervous, my dear sister, the next time there is a little storm or even a great storm. Do not be afraid, my dear friend, when sickness comes into your house. Do not be alarmed, as perhaps you are, when you hear that there is fever next door to you. Remember the promise that precedes our text: "Because thou hast made the LORD, which is my refuge, even the most High, thy habitation; there shall no evil befall thee, neither shall any plague come nigh thy dwelling." But suppose it should seem right to the Lord to let the plague come to you, and suppose you shall die of it, well, you will the sooner be in heaven. Wherefore, comfort one another with the reflection that all is well with you as long as you keep in the way of duty.

And, lastly, *how holy we ought to be with such holy beings watching over us!* If the angels are always hovering around you, mind what you are at. Would you, my dear friend, have spoken as you did when you were coming in at that door yonder if you had seen an angel standing by your side, listening to what you were saying? Oh, no; you are wonderfully decorous when there is somebody near whom you respect! How often your glib tongue is checked when there is some Christian man or woman whom you highly esteem within hearing! How many a thing is done that would not be done under the eye of one whom you love! It is not only true that "a bird of the air shall carry the voice, and that which hath wings shall tell the matter," but it is also true that there are angels watching over us evermore. Paul wrote to the Corinthians that a woman in the public assembly ought to have her head covered because of the angels—a certain decorum was due because of the angels who were there, and I am sure that I may use the same argument concerning all our actions. Whether we are alone or in company, let us not sin because angels are ever watching us, and the angels' Lord is also watching us. May He graciously keep us in His holy way, and if we are so kept, we shall be preserved from all evil while we are here, and at last we shall see His face with joy and abide with Him forever. I would to God that all who are now present were in that holy way. I remind you once more that the entrance to it is by a door that has the blood mark upon the lintel and the two door posts: "The blood shall be to you for a token." "Believe on the Lord Jesus Christ, and thou shalt be saved."

10

Men Chosen—Fallen Angels Rejected

Verily he took not on him the nature of angels; but he took on him the seed of Abraham (Hebrews 2:16).

The Almighty God, who dwelt alone, was pleased to manifest Himself by created works that should display His wisdom and His power. When He set about the mighty work of creation, He determined in His own mind that He would fashion a variety of works and that all His creatures should not be of one form, nature, grandeur, or dignity, hence He made some grains of dust and others mountains of stupendous magnitude; He created some drops and some oceans, some mighty hills and some valleys. Even in His inanimate works He preserved a wonderful variety; He gave not to all stars the same glory, neither to all worlds the same ponderous mass; He gave not to all rocks the same texture, nor to all seas the same shape or fashion, but He was pleased in the work of His hands to observe an infinite variety.

When He came to create living creatures, there, too, are distinctions that we must note. From the worm up to the eagle, from the eagle to the man, from the man to the angel—such are the steps of creating goodness in the fashion of things that are animate. He has not made all creatures eagles, neither has He fashioned all beings worms, but having a right to do what He wills with His own, He has exercised that right in making one creature the majestic lion, king of the forest and another the harmless lamb which shall be devoured without power to resist its enemy or defend itself. He has made His creatures just as it seemed Him fit. He has given to one swiftness of foot, to another, speed of wing; to one, clearness of eye, to another, force of sinew. He

---

This sermon was taken from *The New Park Street Pulpit* and was preached on Sunday evening, June 29, 1856.

has not followed any fixed rule in His creation, but He has done exactly as it pleased Him in the arrangement of the forms that He has animated. So, also, we must observe a great difference in the rational beings that He has created. He has not made all men alike, they differ mightily; from the man of the smallest intellect to the man of majestic mind there are no few steps. And then there is the higher order of rational creatures, more superior to unrenewed man than man ever can be to his fellows, namely, the order of angels. And in the fashioning of angels and men, God again has exercised His own right to create as He pleases, to do just as He wills with His own. Thence, all angels may not be alike in dignity, and all men are not alike in intellect. He has made them to differ.

But now we wish to draw your attention to two instances of God's doing as He pleases in the fashioning of the works of His hands—in the case of angels and in the case of men. Angels were the elder born. God created them, and it pleased Him to give to them a free will to do as they pleased, to choose the good or to prefer the evil, even as He did to man. He gave them this stipulation, that if they should prefer the good, then their station in heaven should be forever fixed and firm, but if they sinned, they should be punished for their guilt and cast out from the presence of His glory into flames of fire. In an evil hour, Satan, one of the chiefs of the angels, rebelled; he tempted others, and he led astray a part of the stars of heaven. God, in His divine vengeance, smote those rebel angels, drove them from their heavenly seats, banished them from their abodes of happiness and glory, and sent them down to dwell forever in the abyss of hell. The rest He confirmed, calling them the elect angels; He made their thrones eternally secure and gave them an entail of those crowns which, sustained by His grace, they had preserved by the rectitude of their holy conduct.

After that it pleased Him to make another race of beings called men. He did not make them all at once; He made but two of them, Adam and Eve, and He committed to their keeping the safety of their entire progeny throughout all generations. He said to Adam, as He had said to the angels, "I give to you free will; you may obey or disobey as you please. There is My law; you are not to touch that tree. The command is by no means irksome. To keep that command will not be difficult to you, for I have given you free will to choose the good." However, so it happened, much to the misery of man, that Adam broke the covenant of works; he ate the accursed fruit, and in that day he fell. Ah! what a fall was there! Then you and I and all of us fell down, while cursed sin did triumph over us; there were no men that stood; there were some angels that stood but no men, for the fall of Adam was the fall of our entire race.

After one portion of the angels had fallen, it pleased God to stamp their doom and make it fast and firm, but when man had fallen, it did not so please God. He had threatened to punish him, but in His infinite mercy He selected the major portion of the human race whom He made the objects of His special affection, for whom He provided a precious remedy, to whom He covenanted salvation and secured it by the blood of His everlasting Son. These are the persons whom we call the elect, and those whom He has let to perish, perish on account of their own sins, most justly, to the praise of His glorious justice. Now, here you notice divine sovereignty—sovereignty in that God chose to put both men and angels on the footing of their free will; sovereignty in that He chose to punish all the fallen angels with utter destruction, sovereignty in that He chose to reprieve the whole human race and to grant an eternal pardon to a number, whom no man can number, selected out of men who shall infallibly be found before His right hand above. My text mentions this great fact, for when properly translated it reads thus: "He took not up angels, but he took on him the seed of Abraham." As this text has two translations, I shall give you the two meanings as briefly as I can.

The Authorized Version

In the first place, the translation of our Authorized Version runs thus: "He took not on him the nature of angels." Our Lord and Savior Jesus Christ, when He came from heaven to die, did not take on Himself the nature of angels. It would have been a stoop more immense than if a seraph should have changed himself into an emmet for the Almighty Son of God to have been clothed in the garb of even the archangel Gabriel, but His condescension dictated to Him that if He did stoop, He would descend to the very lowest degree, that if He did become a creature, He would become not the noblest creature but one of the most ignoble of rational beings, that is to say, man; therefore, *He did not stoop to the intermediate step of angelship, but He stooped right down and became a man.* "He took not on him the nature of angels: but he took on him the seed of Abraham." Let us notice the wisdom and the love of this, and I think there will be something to cause us to glorify God for so doing.

1. In the first place, if Christ had taken upon Himself the nature of angels, *He could never have made an atonement for man.* Setting aside the thought that if He came to save man it would have seemed improper if He had come in the garb of angels, you must allow that if He had done so He could not have seen death. How could angels die? We can suppose that their spirits may become extinct if God should will it; we can suppose the entire annihilation of that to which God alone supplies immortality. But since angels have no bodies, we cannot suppose them capable of death, for death is the separation of the body and the soul.

Therefore, it behooved Christ that He should take upon Himself the form of a man that He might become obedient to death, even the death of the cross. Had angels been standing by, they would have said, "Oh! mighty Master, take our radiant robes. Oh! take not the poor everyday garb of humanity, take our glittering garments all bright with pearls." And Gabriel would have said, "Come, take my wings, mighty Maker, and I shall count myself too honored to have lost them for Your sake. Then, take this crown and this mantle of azure wherewith to clothe Yourself, Son of God. Put my silver sandals on Your feet. Become not man but angel, if You will stoop." But no, He would have said, "Gabriel, if I were in your dress I could not fight with death; I could not sleep in the tomb; I could not feel the pangs and agony of dissolution; therefore, I must, I will, become a man." He took not on Him the nature of angels, but He took on Him the seed of Abraham.

2. Had our Savior become an angel, we must note in the next place that He would never have been a fitting example for us. I cannot imitate an angelic example in all points; it may be very good, so far as I can imitate, but it cannot in all points be my pattern. If you would give me something to imitate, give me a man like myself, then I may attempt to follow him. An angel could not have set us the same holy and pious example that our Savior did. Had He descended from on high in the garb of one of those bright spirits, He might have been a fine example for those brilliant cherubs who surround His throne, but we, poor mortal men condemned to drag the chain of mortality along this earthly existence, would have turned aside and said, "Ah! such a thing is too high for us, we cannot attain to it," and we, therefore, should have stopped short. If I am to carve marble, give me a marble statue that I am to copy, and if this mortal clay is to be cut out into the very model of perfection, as it is to be by God's Spirit, then give me a man for my example, for a man I am, and as a man I am to be made perfect. Not only could not Christ have been a Redeemer, but He could not have been our exemplar if He had taken upon Himself the nature of angels.

3. Sweetly, also, let us remember that if Christ had been an angel, *He could not have sympathized with us.* In order to sympathize with our fellow creatures we must be something like them. Imagine a man made of iron or of brass; could he sympathize with our wearied lungs or with our aching bones? Let such a man be told of sickness or of illness, could he understand it? I would not have him for a nurse, I would not care to have such a being for my physician; he could not feel for me, he could not sympathize with me. No, even our own fellow creatures cannot sympathize with us unless they have suffered as we have done. I have heard of a lady who never knew poverty in all her life, and consequently she could not sympathize with the poor. She heard the

complaint that bread was extremely dear when it was running up to fourteen pence a loaf. "Oh!" she said, "I have no patience with the poor people grumbling about the dearness of bread. If bread is so dear, let them live on penny buns; they are always cheap enough." She had not been in the position of the poor and therefore she could not sympathize with them. No man can sympathize with another to any great extent unless he has been in some measure in the same position and endured the same trouble. It behooved him, therefore, that he should be made in all points like his brethren, that he might be a faithful high priest; "for we have not an high priest which cannot be touched with the feeling of our infirmities; but was in all points tempted like as we are, yet without sin." But if He had been an angel, what sympathy could He have had for me? Suppose I should tell an angel that I could scarcely resist my corruptions, the angel would look at me and wonder what I meant. If I should tell him that I find this world a vast howling wilderness, how could he believe me? He has never heard howlings; his ears have only been saluted by golden harps and sweet choral symphonies of praise. If I should tell him that I found it hard work to hold on my way and keep close to my Savior, the angel could only say, "I cannot sympathize with you, for I am not tempted as you are; I have no clogging nature to abate my ardent zeal, but day without night with unflagging wing I circle His throne rejoicing, nor have I a wish nor will to depart from my great Maker." There you see the Savior's wisdom. He would become a man and not an angel.

4. Once more, Christ became a man and not an angel *because He desired to be one with His dear church.* Christ was betrothed to His church before time began, and when He came into the world He virtually said, "I will go with you, My bride, and I will delight Myself in your company. Angels' garments were not a fitting wedding dress for Me to wear if I am to be bone of your bone and flesh of your flesh. I am allied to you by a union firm and strong. I have called you Hephzibah, my delight is in you; and I have said, your land shall be called Beulah, that is, married. Well, if I am married to you, I will live in the same condition with you; it were not fit that husband should live in palace and that wife should live in cottage; it were not meet that husband should be arrayed in gorgeous robes and wife in meaner garment. No," said He to His church, "if you dwell upon earth, I will; if you dwell in a tabernacle of clay, I will do the same."

> Yea, said the Lord, with her I'll go,
> Through all the depths of care and woe,
> And on the cross will even dare
> The bitter pangs of death to bear.

Christ cannot bear to be different from His church. You know, He would not be in heaven without her, therefore did He make that long, long journey to redeem her and visit her, and when He came on this good errand, He would not that she should be made of clay and He should not be made of clay too; He was the head, and it would have been out of order that the head should have been of gold and the body of clay; it would have been like Nebuchadnezzar's image that must be broken. Since the children were partakers of flesh and blood, He must also take part in the same, for He became "perfect through sufferings," since He was the captain of our salvation. Thus, again, you see His love and His wisdom that He took not on him the nature of angels, but took upon him the seed of Abraham.

5. If Christ had not taken upon Him the nature of man, then *manhood would not have been so honorable or so comfortable as it is.* I consider that to be a Christian man is to be the greatest thing that God has made. Little as I am, I can say of myself if I am a child of God, I am next to my Maker. There is an infinite, an awful, an immeasurable distance, but, save Jesus Christ Himself, there is no being between man and God. As for an angel, he is less than redeemed man. Are they not ministering spirits, sent forth to be ministers to us who are heirs of salvation? Without controversy, the less is minister to the greater, and the greater shall not attend the less; therefore, the angels are less than men, for they minister to us. Manhood is a noble thing, for God wore manhood once; manhood is a glorious thing, for it was the robe of the eternal; God was made flesh and dwelt among us. Therefore, flesh is dignified and glorified. As I said, it would not be so comfortable to be a man if Christ had not been a man, for I know that I must die. Now my comfort is that I shall rise again, but I should not have had that comfort if Christ had not been a man and if He had not died and risen again. Oh! death, I have often seen your dungeon, and I have thought, how can it be that any should escape therefrom. The walls thereof are thick, and against the door is a ponderous stone. It is sealed fast, and watchers guard it. Oh! death, where is the man that can rend your sepulcher or open your door? Your iron bars, O death, cannot be filed by mortal, and your chains are too heavy to be snapped by the finite, but I take comfort for there was *a man* who broke the bonds of death; there was one who snapped the fetter, cut the bars of brass, unlocked the gates, and made His way triumphant through the sky; in that man I see an instance of what I, too, shall do. When the loud trump of the archangel shall startle my sleeping atoms, I, too, shall find it easy to rise, for as the Lord my Savior rose, so all His followers must. Therefore, death, I look upon your dungeon as one that must be opened again, for it has been opened once. I look upon your worm as but a little thing that must yield

up its prey and give back the flesh whereon it fed. I look upon the stone of your sepulcher as but some pebble of ocean's shingly beach which I shall cast away with eager hand when I shall burst the cerements of the grave and mount to immortality. It is a comfortable thing to be a man because Christ died and rose again, but had He been an angel, the resurrection would not have had that great and glorious proof, nor should we have been so content to be human seeing there would be death but no immortality and life.

The Literal Translation

Thus I have tried to explain the first part of the subject, and now for the second: The literal translation, according to the marginal reading, is *"He took not up angels, but he took up the seed of Abraham,"* by which is meant that Christ did not die to save angels, though many of them needed salvation, but He died to save fallen man. Now, I like every now and then to give the opponents of the great doctrines of grace something hard to put between their teeth. I have often been told that election is a most dreadful doctrine and to teach that God saves some and lets others perish is to make God unjust. Sometimes I have asked how that was, and the usual answer I have gotten is this: Suppose a father should have a certain number of children and he were to put some of his children into a terrible dungeon and make the rest of them happy, would you think that father was just? Well, I reply, you have supposed a case, and I will answer you. Of course I should not; the child has a claim upon his father, and the father is bound to give him his claim. But I want to know what you mean by asking that question. How does that apply to the case of God? I did not know that all men were God's children; I knew that they were God's rebellious subjects, but I did not know that they were His children. I thought they did not become His children until they were born again, and that when they were His children, He did treat them all alike and did carry them all to heaven and give them all a mansion. I never did hear that He sent any of His children to hell. True, I have heard *you* say so; I have heard *you* say that some of His children fall from grace, and He therefore sends them to hell, and I leave you to solve the problem how that is just. But, sir, I do not allow that all God's creatures are His children.

I have got a small question for you. How do you explain this—that the devils and fallen angels are all lost, and yet, according to your own showing, fallen men all have a chance of being saved? How do you make that out? "Oh!" say you, "that is a different matter; I was not calculating about the fallen angels." But if you were to ask the Devil about it, he would not tell you it was a different matter; he would say, "Sir, if all men are God's children, all devils are quite as much so. I am sure they ought to stand on the same footing as men, and a fallen angel has as much right to call himself one of God's children as a fallen man." And I should like you to answer the Devil on that subject on your own hypothesis. Let Satan, for once, ask you a question, "You say it is unfair of God to send one of His children to hell and take another to heaven. Now, you have said all creatures are His children. Well, I am a creature, and, therefore, I am His child. I want to know, my friend," says Satan, "how you make it just that my Father should send me to hell and let you go to heaven?" Now, you must settle that question with the Devil; I will not answer for you. I never supposed such a case. My views never bring me into such a dilemma, but you are in for the trouble, and you may get out of it the best way you can.

On my principle, the deed is just enough; men and devils have both sinned and have both deserved to be damned for their sins. God, if He shall so resolve, can justly destroy them all, or He may save them all, if He can do it with justice, or He may save one of them if He pleases and let the others perish. If as He has done, He chooses to save a remnant and that remnant shall be men, and if He allows all the fallen angels to sink to hell, all that we can answer is that God is just, and He has a right to do as He pleases with His creatures. You know, you give to the queen the right to pardon a rebel when she sees fit, and will you not give that right to God? "No," say you, "not unless He pardons all." Well, sir, then there were no right at all in that. The queen would not thank you if you gave her liberty to pardon all; she would say, "No, there are instances where it is to my honor and to the honor of my laws not to pardon, and, therefore, I will not do it. There are other instances where it is to the honor of my clemency and not hurtful to my laws and, therefore, these I pardon, and I uphold my right to do it." Now, what you will give to a king or an emperor you will deny to God, but I stand here to claim this right for Him. Deny it if you please; you will have to deny it in the teeth of the Scriptures, for they do authoritatively declare that God is a Sovereign, that He has "mercy on whom he will have mercy, and whom he will he hardeneth."

Now, come, if our friend will let us, we will for a moment just consider this case: how it is that devils are lost and some men are saved?

1. In the first place, *I do not think it is because of any difference in the sin.* When two criminals are brought before a judge, if one of them is to be saved and the other punished, very likely the judge will say, "Which is the greatest offender? Let the great offender die, and let the lesser offender be saved." Now, I do not know that Satan was a greater offender than man; I am not sure that the fallen angels sinned more than man did. "Why sir," you say, "man's sin was a very little one; he only stole some of his Master's fruit." Aye, but if it was such a little thing to

do, what a little thing it would have been not to do it! If it were so little a thing, how easily he might have avoided it! And, therefore, because he did it, it became all the greater sin. "Oh!" you say, "but Satan was proud, and the fallen angels were proud." And are *you* not pretty tolerably in the same direction my friend? At any rate, Adam was. "But," you say, "Satan was rebellious." Well if *you* were not a rebel, you would not talk so; if you had not rebelled against God, you would not set yourself up to deny His sovereignty. "But," you say, "the Devil was a liar from the beginning." I wonder how long it is since *you* have spoken the truth, sir; you know how to lie as well as he, and though you may not have developed your sin as much as the fallen angels have done, if God were to let you alone and take the curb off, I wonder what would be the difference between you and the Devil. I believe that if men were allowed to do just as they liked and there were no government over them, they would almost go beyond Satan. Look at Robespierre in France; look at the doings of the Reign of Terror; turn to heathen countries; I dare not tell you in public what abominable vices, what lascivious sins are committed there. I point you to Sodom and Gomorrah, and I ask you what may man become, and I say that I do not know but that a man might become as vile as a devil if God's restraining mercy were taken from him. At any rate I do not say but that Adam's sin was as great as Satan's. "Ah!" you say, "but Adam was tempted to do it." Yes, that was some excuse, but so were the greater part of the devils. It is true, Satan was not tempted, he did it of his own free will, but he tempted the other spirits, and, therefore, the excuse that will do for man will do for the great mass of fallen spirits. Why did not God, therefore, select a portion of the fallen spirits to be saved? I answer that you can never find any reason except this, Shall I not do what I will with mine own? We must fall down and breathlessly admire the infinite sovereignty that passed by angels and saved men.

2. But suppose there is not much difference in their sin, the next question is *which of those two beings is the most worth saving?* Which is the most valuable creature? Which would serve his Maker most, if his Maker should spare him? And I defy any of you to hold that a sinful man is a more valuable creature than an angel. Why, if God had looked at profit, speaking after the manner of men, it would be more profitable to Him to save the angel. Could not the restored angel serve Him better than the restored man? If I serve God day after day, yet at night I must rest, but the angels serve day without night in His temple. If my zeal be ever so intense, yet my body must flag, but angels know not weariness, and if saved, I shall make but a poor courtier to stand around His throne, but yon bright fallen seraph would, if he had been delivered, have made a very peer to grace the halls of the Almighty. If I shall ever

be carried to heaven, I have no bright angelic honors, and my nature, when ennobled will not surpass what an angel might have been if God had so decreed. If Satan had been saved, oh! how loudly would he have sung, and with what glory would he have marched through heaven to the praise and glory of the grace which rescued him from hell! Therefore, if God had in that thought of His own profit, He would sooner have saved angels than have saved men.

3. Another thought. Sometimes the government will say, "Well, here are two persons to be executed; we desire to save one; *which of the two would be the most dangerous character to allow to continue an enemy?*" Now, which could hurt God the most, speaking as man would speak, a fallen angel or a man? I answer that fallen man can do but little injury to divine government compared to a fallen angel. A fallen angel is so subtle, so powerful, so swift, so able to fly on the lightning's wings that he can do ten times more injury to his Maker, if indeed his Maker can be injured, than ever man could do, so that if there had been any consideration of this kind in the divine mind, God would have selected the devils to save, since they could, if saved, do Him the most glory and if not saved, do Him the most injury.

4. And yet one more consideration here, to show you still further how sovereign is the divine will in this matter. Perhaps it would be said if one is to be saved, let that one be saved who would take the least trouble to save. Now, which could be saved with the greatest ease, should you suppose, a fallen angel or a fallen man? For my part, I can see no difference, but if there be any, it strikes me that a restoration does not put things one-half so much out of order as a revolution, and to have restored the angels to the place from which they had fallen, speaking as a man must speak, would not have been so hard as to have taken fallen man out of the place to which he had fallen and placed him where fallen angels had once stood.

If Satan had entered heaven, it would have been like a restoration— an old king come back to his ancient throne, but when a man goes there, it is like a king going to a new dynasty—a new kingdom. It is the man entering into the angel's place, and for that you know there must be sanctifying grace and purchasing love. That might have been needed for fallen angels, but certainly not more for them than for fallen man. Here, then, we are brought back to the one and only answer—that God saves men and not angels just because He chooses to do it, and He says to angels who have perished, No but, O Satan, who are you that replies against God? Shall the thing formed say to Him that formed it, why have you made me thus?

5. But, you may say, *God saved men because He pitied them.* But then why did He not pity the devils? I know two men living on three or

four shillings a week. I pity one of them very much, indeed, but the
other, who is no better off, I pity the most, for he once knew better
times. Man, it is true, fell out of Eden, but Satan fell out of heaven and
is the more to be pitied on account of the greatness of his fall; therefore,
if pity had ruled the day, God would have decided for the fallen angels
and not for fallen men.

But I think I hear someone whispering again, "Aye, but I do not see
that first part; you said that you did not know but the sin of man was as
great as the sin of Satan." Well, I beg to repeat it, and I say another
thing that, mighty wise as you may be, you do not know any difference
either; do you think if the sins were different the punishment would be
the same? Certainly not, you say—the same punishment for the same
sin. Well, now, devils and men are to be in the same hell; the lake of fire
that was prepared for the Devil and his angels is the place into which
men are cast, and therefore I defy you to prove that their sin is not the
same. I believe, if it be not the same in degree, it is the same in quality
and the same in nature. And, therefore, a fallen angel and a fallen man
stand on a par, so that if God makes a difference, He makes it only because He will make it and gives no account of His dealings. This is a
knife that cuts up root and branch—everything is of like merit; it takes
away from the free-willer any chance of charging God with injustice,
for how can he prove God unjust in saving one man and not another,
when he dares not hint that He is unjust in saving some men and letting
devils perish?

And now I have closed this subject, and I must just make a practical
reflection or so, and then I shall have done. Some may rail at this doc-
trinal preaching and they will go out and call me an antinomian. I will
not be at all particular about that so long as I can make them angry, for
if a man hates the truth I shall never be backward in stirring up his
wrath, and if any man offends my God, then let him be offended. Far
better for him to show his opposition, for then, perhaps, he may know
that it is in him and repent of it before God. But I will show you that
this is a practical subject. It is practical in this way: that if any man does
not submit to God's right to do with him as He pleases, he has very
grave reason to doubt his own piety. "Aye," you say, "too cutting by
half." Now, I do not mean to say anything harsh or bigoted, but I do
mean to say that again. I do not assert that if you doctrinally deny it, but
that if you in your heart hate the doctrine that God has a right to save or
to destroy you, you give me very grave cause to suspect whether you
ever knew your own position in the sight of God. I am quite sure that no
humble sinner will doubt God's right to destroy him, and I believe that
no man who has any love to his fellow creatures, believing that God has
a right to destroy him, will ever quarrel with God if He chose to save

another who is only as bad as himself. I tell you it is your unhumbled pride that kicks against these doctrines; it is your infernal self-conceit, born of hell, that makes you hate this truth. Men have always kicked at it, and they always will. When Christ preached it once, they would have dragged Him out to the brow of the hill and cast Him down headlong. I expect always to meet with opposition if I speak out broadly and plainly, but let me tell you solemnly, if you do not believe God's right over you, I am afraid your heart has never been right before God.

But there is another practical conclusion. If you do feel this to be true, that God has a right to send your soul to hell and that if He saves another and not you He will be just, but if He saves you it will be an act of free distinguishing love, you show a spirit that is very near to the kingdom of heaven. I do not think a man will admit this truth unless he has a change of heart. He may admit it in his mind, but he will not feel it to be true unless he has gotten a new heart and a right spirit. I will not go so far as to say that a man who believes divine sovereignty must be a Christian—that were to stretch the truth, but I do say that if a man is humble enough, meek enough, contrite enough to lay himself down at the Savior's feet with this, "Nothing in my hands I bring"; I have no righteousness, no claims; if You should damn me, You would be just; if You save me, I will thank you forever, such a man must have had a work of grace in his heart to bring him to such a conclusion. If you can say that, then, poor sinner, come to Jesus, come to Jesus, for He will never cast you out.

Let me tell you a story about the prodigal, and then I will be done. The prodigal set out one morning, and he had a long, long journey to go; he had a high hill to climb called the hill of his own sins and follies. He had scarcely got to the top of it and was getting near the tower, called the tower of true repentance, when his father, who was sitting on the top of the house, saw him, and when he saw him, he ran out immediately, and before his son had got to the door, he had fallen on his neck and kissed him. He took his son into his house, and a feast was prepared, and they sat down to it. But after the son had sat down, the father turned his eye to him, and he was not eating, but the tears were rolling down his cheeks. "My son," said the father, "why don't you eat? Why do you weep, my son? The feast is all prepared for you." Bursting into tears, the son said, "Father, do you forgive me all?" "Yes," said the father, "I do. Eat my son. Do not weep." The prodigal went on. The father turned his eye to the other guests, and by and by, looking on his son, he saw that he was weeping again and not eating. Said the father, "Son, why don't you eat? The feast is all for you. Why do you weep, my son?" "Father," said he, with the tears rolling down his cheeks again, "will you let me stay here?" "Oh, yes, my son, said the father, "eat; do not weep; you shall stay here; you are my beloved son." Well, the prodigal went on, and the father looked at the other guests, but by and by he turned his eyes again, and there was his son weeping once more. "My dear son," he asks, "why do you weep?" "Oh, father," said he, "will you *keep* me here? for if you do not, I know I shall run away. Father, will you *make* me stop here?" "Yes, my son," said he, "that I will."

> My grace shall like a fetter bind
> That wandering heart to me.

The son wiped his eyes, went on with his meal, and never wept again. There, poor prodigal, there is something for you; if you will come to Christ, you shall always stay there, and over and above that, He will keep you there. Therefore rejoice, for though He has a right to destroy you, recollect, He will not, for His heart is full of love and pity toward you. Only come to Him, and you shall be saved.

11

The Sympathy of the Two Worlds

There is joy in the presence of the angels of God over one sinner that repenteth (Luke 15:10).

Man's heart is never big enough to hold either its joys or its sorrows. You never heard of a man whose heart was exactly full of sorrow, for no sooner is it full than it overflows. The first prompting of the soul is to tell its sorrow to another. The reason is that our hearts are not large enough to hold our grief; we need to have another heart to receive a portion thereof. It is even so with our joy. When the heart is full of joy, it always allows its joy to escape. It is like the fountain in the marketplace; whenever it is full, it runs away in streams, and so soon as it ceases to overflow, you may be quite sure that it has ceased to be full. The only full heart is the overflowing heart. You know this, beloved, you have proved it to be true, for when your soul has been full of joy, you have first called together your own kindred and friends, and you have communicated to them the cause of your gladness. And when those vessels have been full even to the brim, you have been like the woman who borrowed empty vessels of her neighbors, for you have asked each of them to become partakers in your joy, and when the hearts of all your neighbors have been full, you have felt as if they were not large enough, and the whole world has been called upon to join in your praise. You bade the fathomless ocean drink in your joy; you spoke to the trees and bade them clap their hands while the mountains and hills were invoked by you to break forth into singing; the very stars of heaven seemed to look down upon you, and you bade them sing for you, and all the world was full of

---

This sermon was taken from *The New Park Street Pulpit* and was preached on Sunday morning, July 4, 1858.

music through the music that was in your heart. And, after all, what is man but the great musician of the world? The universe is a great organ with mighty pipes. Space, time, eternity are like the throats of this great organ, and man, a little creature, puts his fingers on the keys and wakes the universe to thunders of harmony, stirring up the whole creation to mightiest acclamations of praise. Know you not that man is God's high priest in the universe? All things else are the sacrifice, but he is the priest—carrying in his heart the fire and in his hand the wood and in his mouth the two-edged sword of dedication with which he offers up all things to God.

But I have no doubt, beloved, the thought has sometimes struck us that our praise does not go far enough. We seem as if we dwelt in an isle cut off from the mainland. This world, like a fair planet, swims in a sea of ether unnavigated by mortal ship. We have sometimes thought that surely our praise was confined to the shores of this poor, narrow world, that it was impossible for us to pull the ropes that might ring the bells of heaven, that we could by no means whatever reach our hands so high as to sweep the celestial chords of angelic harps. We have said to ourselves there is no connection between earth and heaven. A huge black wall divides us. A strait of unnavigable waters shuts us out. Our prayers cannot reach to heaven, neither can our praises affect the celestials. Let us learn from our text how mistaken we are. We are, after all, however much we seem to be shut out from heaven and from the great universe, but a province of God's vast, united empire, and what is done on earth is known in heaven, what is sung on earth is sung in heaven, and there is a sense in which it is true that the tears of earth are wept again in paradise, and the sorrows of mankind are felt again, even on the throne of the Most High.

My text tells us, "There is joy in the presence of the angels of God over one sinner that repenteth." It seems as if it showed me a bridge by which I might cross over into eternity. It does, as it were, exhibit to me certain magnetic wires that convey the intelligence of what is done here to spirits in another world. It teaches me that there is a real and wonderful connection between this lower world and that which is beyond the skies where God dwells in the land of the happy.

We shall talk about that subject a little this morning. My first head will be *the sympathy of the world above with the world below*; the second, *the judgment of the angels*—they rejoice over repenting sinners; we shall see what is their ground for so doing. The third will be *a lesson for the saints*; if the angels in heaven rejoice over repenting sinners, so should we.

The Sympathy of the Two Worlds

Imagine not, O son of man, that you are cut off from heaven, for there is a ladder, the top whereof does rest at the foot of the throne of the Almighty, the base whereof is fixed in the lowest place of man's misery! Conceive not that there is a great gulf fixed between you and the Father across which His mercy cannot come and over which your prayers and faith can never leap. Oh, think not, son of man, that you dwell in a storm-girt island cut off from the continent of eternity. I beseech you, believe that there is a bridge across that chasm, a road along which feet may travel. This world is not separated, for all creation is but one body. And know then, O son of man, though you in this world do but dwell as it were on the foot, yet from the feet even to the head there are nerves and veins that do unite the whole. The same great heart that beats in heaven beats on earth. The love of the Eternal Father that cheers the celestial makes glad the terrestrial too. Rest assured that though the glory of the celestial is one and the glory of the terrestrial is another, yet are they but another in appearance, for after all, they are the same. Oh! listen, son of man, and you will soon learn that you are no stranger in a strange land—a houseless Joseph in the land of Egypt, shut out from his father and his brothers, who still remain in the happy paradise of Canaan. No, your Father loves you still. There is a connection between you and Him. Strange that though leagues of distance lie between the finite creature and the infinite Creator, yet there are links that unite us! When a tear is wept by you, think not your Father does not behold, for, "Like as a father pitieth his children, so the LORD pitieth them that fear him." Your sigh is able to move the heart of Jehovah, your whisper can incline His ear to you, your prayer can stay His hands, your faith can move His arm. Oh! think not that God sits on high in an eternal slumber, taking no account of you. "Can a woman forget her sucking child, that she should not have compassion on the son of her womb? yea, they may forget, yet will I not forget thee." Engraven upon the Father's hand your name remains, and on His heart recorded there your person stands. He thought of you before the worlds were made; before the channels of the sea were scooped or the gigantic mountains lifted their heads in the white clouds, He thought of you. He thinks on you still. "I the LORD do keep it; I will water it every moment: lest any hurt it, I will keep it night and day." For the eyes of the Lord run to and fro in every place, to show Himself strong on the behalf of all them that fear Him. You are not cut off from Him. You do move in Him; in Him you do live and have your being. He is a very present help in time of trouble.

Remember, O heir of immortality, that you are not only linked to the Godhead, but there is another one in heaven with whom you have a strange yet near connection. In the center of the throne sits one who is your brother, allied to you by blood. *The Son of God*, eternal, equal with His Father, became in the fullness of time the Son of Mary, an infant of a span long. He was, yes is, bone of your bone and flesh of your flesh. Think not that you are cut off from the celestial world while He is there, for is He not your head, and has He not Himself declared that you are a member of His body, of His flesh, and of His bones? Oh, man, you are not separated from heaven while Jesus tells you—

> I feel at my heart all thy sighs and thy groans,
> For thou art most near me, my flesh and my bones,
> In all thy distresses, thy Head feels the pain,
> They all are most needful, not one is in vain.

Oh, poor, disconsolate mourner, Christ remembers you every hour. Your sighs are His sighs, your groans are His groans, your prayers are His prayers.

> He in his measure feels afresh,
> What every member bears.

Crucified He is when you are crucified; He dies when you die; you live in Him, and He lives in you, and because He lives shall you live also; you shall rise in Him, and you shall sit together in the heavenly places with Him. Oh, never was husband nearer to his wife and never head nearer to the members and never soul nearer to the body of this flesh than Christ is to you, and while it is so, think not that heaven and earth are divided. They are but kindred worlds, two ships moored close to one another; one short plank of death will enable you to step from one into the other; this ship, all black and coaly, having done the coasting trade, the dusty business of today, and being full of the blackness of sorrow; that ship all golden, with its painted pennon flying and its sail all spread, white as the down of the seabird, fair as the angel's wing. I tell you, man, the ship of heaven is moored side-by-side with the ship of earth, and rock though this ship may and careen though she will on stormy winds and tempests, yet the invisible and golden ship of heaven sails by her side never sundered, never divided, always ready in order that when the hour shall come, you may leap from the black, dark ship and step upon the golden deck of that thrice happy one in which you shall sail forever.

But, O man of God, there are other golden links besides this that bind the present to the future and time to eternity. And what are time and eternity, after all, to the believer, but like the Siamese twins, never to be separated? This earth is heaven below, the next world is but a heaven above; it is the same house—this is the lower room and that the upper, but the same roof covers both, and the same dew falls upon each. Remember, beloved, that *the spirits of the just made perfect* are never far from you and me if we are lovers of Jesus. All those who have passed the flood have still communion with us. Do we not sing—

> The saints on earth, and all the dead,
> But one communion make;
> All join in Christ, the living Head,
> And of his grace partake.

We have but one Head for the church triumphant and for the church militant:

> One army of the living God,
> To his command we bow;
> Part of the host have cross'd the flood,
> And part are crossing now.

Does not the apostle tell us that the saints above are a cloud of witnesses? After he had mentioned Abraham and Isaac and Jacob and Gideon and Barak and Jephthah, did he not say, "Wherefore seeing we also are compassed about with so great a cloud of witnesses, let us lay aside every weight." Lo, we are running in the plains, and the glorified ones are looking down upon us. Your mother's eyes follow you, young man; a father's eyes are looking down upon you, young woman. The eyes of my godly grandmother, long since glorified, I doubt not rest on me perpetually. No doubt in heaven they often talk of us. I think they sometimes visit this poor earth—they never go out of heaven, it is true, for heaven is everywhere to them. This world is to them but just one corner of God's heaven, one shady bower of paradise.

The saints of the living God are, I doubt not, very near to us, when we think them very far away. At any rate, they still remember us, still look for us, for this is ever upon their hearts—the truth that they without us cannot be made perfect. They cannot be a perfect church until we are gathered in, and therefore do they long for our appearing.

But to come to our text a little more minutely, it assures us that the angels have communion with us. Bright spirits, firstborn sons of God, do you think of me? Oh, cherubim great and mighty, seraphim burning, winged with lightning, do you think of us? Gigantic is your stature. Our poet tells us that the wand of an angel might make a mast for some tall admiral, and doubtless he was right when he said so. Those angels of God are creatures mighty and strong, doing His commandments, hearkening to His word—and do they take notice of us? Let the Scripture answer, "Are they not all ministering spirits, sent forth to minister for them who shall be heirs of salvation?" "The angel of the LORD encampeth round about them that fear him." "For he shall give his angels charge over thee, to keep thee in all thy ways. They shall bear thee up in their hands, lest thou dash thy foot against a stone." Yes, the brightest angels are but the serving men of the saints; they are our lacqueys and our footmen. They wait upon us, they are the troops of our bodyguard, and we might, if our eyes were opened, see what Elisha saw, horses of fire and chariots of fire round about us, so that we should joyously say, "They that be with us are more than they that be with them."

Our text tells us that the angels of God rejoice over repenting sinners. How is that? They are always as happy as they can be; how can they be any happier? The text does not say that they are any happier, but perhaps that they show their happiness more. A man may have a Sabbath every day, as he ought to have if he is a Christian, and yet on the first day of the week he will let his Sabbatism come out plainly, for then the world shall see that he does rest. "A merry heart hath a continual feast"; but then even the merry heart has some special days on which it feasts well. To the glorified every day is a Sabbath, but of some it can be said, "That sabbath day was an high day." There are days when the angels sing more loudly than usual; they are always harping well God's praise, but sometimes the gathering hosts who have been flitting far through the universe come home to their center, and around the throne of God, standing in serried ranks, marshaled not for battle but for music, on certain set and appointed days they chant the praise of the Son of God, who loved us and gave himself for us. And do you ask me when those days occur? I tell you, the birthday of every Christian is a sonnet day in heaven. There are Christmas days in paradise, where Christ's high mass is kept, and Christ is glorified not because He was born in a manger but because He is born in a broken heart. There are days—good days in heaven, days of sonnet, red letter days of overflowing adoration. And these are days when the shepherd brings home the lost sheep upon His shoulder, when the church has swept her house and found the lost piece of money, for then are these friends and neighbors called together, and they rejoice with joy unspeakable and full of glory over one sinner that repents.

I have thus, I hope, shown you that there is a greater connection between earth and heaven than any of us dreamed. And now let none of us think, when we look upward to the blue sky, that we are far from heaven; it is a very little distance from us. When the day comes, we shall go posthaste there, even without horses and chariots of fire. Balaam called it a land that is very far off; we know better—it is a land that is very near. Even now,

> By faith we join our hands
> With those that went before,
> And greet the blood-besprinkled bands
> Upon the eternal shore.

All hail, bright spirits! I see you now. All hail, angels! All hail, you brethren redeemed! A few more hours or days or months and we shall join your happy throng; until then your joyous fellowship, your sweet compassion shall ever be our comfort and our consolation—and having weathered all storms of life, we shall at last anchor with you within the port of everlasting peace.

The Judgment of the Angels

Why do angels sing over penitent sinners? In the first place, I think it is because they remember the days of creation. You know, when God made this world and fixed the beams of the heavens in sockets of light, the morning stars sang together, and the sons of God shouted for joy; as they saw star after star flying abroad like sparks from the great anvil of Omnipotence, they began to sing; every time they saw a new creature made upon this little earth, they praised afresh. When first they saw light, they clapped their hands and said, "Great is Jehovah; for He said 'Light be!' and light was." And when they saw sun and moon and stars, again they clapped their hands, and they said, He has "made great lights: for his mercy endureth forever: The sun to rule by day: for his mercy endureth forever: The moon . . . to rule by night: for his mercy endureth forever." And over everything He made, they chanted evermore that sweet song, "Creator, you are to be magnified, for your mercy endureth forever." Now, when they see a sinner returning, they see the creation over again, for repentance is a new creation. No man ever repents until God makes in him a new heart and a right spirit. I do not know that ever since the day when God made the world, with the exception of new hearts, the angels have seen God make anything else. He may, if He has so pleased, have made fresh worlds since that time. But perhaps the only instance of new creation they have ever seen since the first day is the creation of a new heart and a right spirit within the breast of a poor penitent sinner. Therefore do they sing because creation comes over again.

I doubt not, too, that they sing because they behold God's works afresh shining in excellence. When God first made the world, He said of it, "It is very good"—He could not say so now. There are many of you that God could not say that of. He would have to say the very reverse. He would have to say, "No, that is very bad, for the trail of the serpent has swept away your beauty, that moral excellence which once dwelt in manhood has passed away"; but when the sweet influences of the Spirit bring men to repentance and faith again, God looks upon man, and He says, "It is very good." For what His Spirit makes is like Himself—good and holy and precious, and God smiles again over His twice-made creation and says once more, "It is very good." Then the angels begin again and praise His name whose works are always good and full of beauty.

But, beloved, the angels sing over sinners that repent because they know what that poor sinner has escaped. You and I can never imagine all the depths of hell. Shut out from us by a black veil of darkness, we cannot tell the horrors of that dismal dungeon of lost souls. Happily, the wailings of the damned have never startled us, for a thousand tempests were but a maiden's whisper compared with one wail of a damned spirit. It is not possible for us to see the tortures of those souls who dwell eternally within an anguish that knows no alleviation. These eyes would become sightless balls of darkness if they were permitted for an instant to look into that ghastly shrine of torment. Hell is horrible, for we may say of it, eye has not seen, nor ear heard, neither has it entered into the heart of man to conceive the horrors that God has prepared for them that hate Him. But the angels know better than you or I could guess. They know it; not that they have felt it, but they remember that day when Satan and his angels rebelled against God. They remember the day when the third part of the stars of heaven revolted against their liege Lord, and they have not forgotten how the red right hand of Jehovah Jesus was wrapped in thunder. They do not forget that breach in the battlements of heaven when, down from the greatest heights to the lowest depths, Lucifer and his hosts were hurled. They have never forgotten how with sound of trumpet they pursued the flying foe down to the gulfs of black despair; and, as they neared that place where the great serpent is to be bound in chains, they remember how they saw Tophet, which was prepared of old, the pile whereof is fire and much wood. And they recollect how, when they winged back their flight, every tongue was silent, although they might well have shouted the praise of Him who conquered Lucifer, but on them all there did sit a solemn awe of one who could smite a cherub and cast him into hopeless bonds of everlasting despair. They knew what hell was, for they had looked within its jaws and had seen their own brothers fast enclosed within them; therefore, when they see a sinner saved they rejoice because there is one less to be food for the never dying worm—one more soul escaped out of the mouth of the lion.

There is yet a better reason. The angels know what the joys of heaven are, and therefore, they rejoice over one sinner that repents. We talk about pearly gates and golden streets and white robes and harps of gold and crowns of amaranth and all that; but if an angel could speak to us of heaven, he would smile and say, "All those fine things are but child's talk, and you are little children, and you cannot understand the greatness of eternal bliss, and therefore God has given you a child's hornbook and an alphabet in which you may learn the first rough letters of what heaven is, but what it is you do not know. O mortal, your eye has never yet beheld its splendors, your ear has never yet been ravished with its melodies, your heart has never been transported with its peerless joys." You may talk and think and guess and dream, but you must never measure the infinite heaven that God has provided for His children, and therefore it is when they see a soul saved and a sinner repenting that they clap their hands, for they know that all those blessed mansions are theirs, since all those sweet places of everlasting happiness are the entail of every sinner that repents.

But I want you just to read the text again, while I dwell upon another thought. There is joy in the presence of the angels of God over one sinner *that repenteth*. Now, why do they not save their joy until that sinner dies and goes to heaven? Why do they rejoice over him when he repents? My Arminian friend, I think, ought to go to heaven to set them right upon this matter. According to his theory, it must be very wrong of them because they rejoice prematurely. According to the Arminian doctrine, a man may repent, and yet he may be lost; he may have grace to repent and believe, and yet he may fall from grace and be a castaway. Now, angels, don't be too fast. Perhaps you may have to repent of this one day if the Arminian doctrine is true; I would advise you to save your song for greater joys. Why, angels, perhaps the men that you are singing over today you will have to mourn over tomorrow. I am quite sure that Arminius never taught his doctrine in heaven. I do not know whether he is there—I hope he is, but he is no longer an Arminian. But if he ever taught his doctrine there, he would be put out. The reason why angels rejoice is because they know that when a sinner repents, he is absolutely saved—or else they would rejoice prematurely and would have good cause for retracting their merriment on some future occasion. But the angels know what Christ meant when He said, "I give unto them eternal life; and they shall never perish, neither shall any man pluck them out of my hand"; therefore they rejoice over repenting sinners because they know they are saved.

There is yet one more fact I will mention before I leave this point. It is said that the angels rejoice over *one* sinner that repenteth. Now this evening it shall be my happy privilege to give the right hand of fellowship to no less than forty-eight sinners that have repented, and there will be great joy and rejoicing in our churches tonight because these forty-eight have been immersed on a profession of their faith. But how loving are the angels to men, for they rejoice over *one* sinner that repents. There she is in that garret where the stars look between the tiles. There is a miserable bed in that room with but one bit of covering, and she lies there to die! Poor creature! many a night she has walked the streets in the time of her merriment, but now her joys are over; a foul disease, like a demon, is devouring her heart! She is dying fast, and no one cares for her soul! But there in that chamber she turns her face to the wall, and she cries, "O You that saved Magdalene, save me; Lord, I repent, have mercy upon me, I beseech You." Did the bells ring in the street? Was the trumpet blown? Ah! no. Did men rejoice? Was there a sound of thanksgiving in the midst of the great congregation? No, no one heard it, for she died unseen. But stay! There was one standing at her bedside who noted well that tear—an angel who had come down from heaven to watch over this stray sheep and mark its return, and no sooner was her prayer uttered than he clapped his wings, and there was seen flying up to the pearly gates a spirit like a star. The heavenly guards came crowding to the gate, crying, "What news, O son of fire?" He said, "'Tis done." "And what is done?" they said. "Why, she has repented." "What! she who was once a chief of sinners? Has she turned to Christ?" "'Tis even so," said he. And then they told it through the streets, and the bells of heaven rang marriage peals, for Magdalene was saved, and she who had been the chief of sinners was turned to the living God.

It was in another place. A poor neglected little boy in ragged clothing had run about the streets for many days. Tutored in crime, he was paving his path to the gallows; but one morning he passed by a humble room where some men and women were sitting together teaching poor ragged children. He stopped in there, a wild Bedouin of the streets; they talked to him; they told him about a soul and about an eternity—things he had never heard before; they spoke of Jesus and of good tidings of great joy to this poor friendless lad. He went another Sabbath and another, his wild habits hanging about him, for he could not got rid of them. At last it happened that his teacher said to him one day, "Jesus Christ receives sinners." That little boy ran, but not home, for it was but a mockery to call it so—where a drunken father and a lascivious mother kept a hellish riot together. He ran, and under some dry arch or in some wild unfrequented corner he bent his little knees, and there he cried, that poor creature in his rags, "Lord save me, or I perish"; and the little urchin was on his knees—the little thief was saved! He said—"Jesus, lover of my soul, let me to your bosom fly."

And up from that old arch, from that forsaken hovel, there flew a spirit glad to bear the news to heaven that another heir of glory was born to God. I might picture many such scenes, but will each of you try to picture your own? You remember the occasion when the Lord met with you. Ah! little did you think what a commotion there was in heaven. If the queen had ordered out all her soldiers, the angels of heaven would not have stopped to notice them; if all the princes of earth had marched in pageant through the streets, with all their robes and jewelry and crowns and all their regalia and their chariots and their horsemen—if the pomps of ancient monarchies had risen from the tomb—if all the might of Babylon and Tyre and Greece had been concentrated into one great parade, yet not an angel would have stopped in his course to smile at those poor tawdry things; but over you, the vilest of the vile, the poorest of the poor, the most obscure and unknown—over you angelic wings were hovering, and concerning you it was said on earth and sung in heaven, "Hallelujah, for a child is born to God today."

A Lesson to the Saints

I think, beloved, the lesson will not be hard for you to learn. The angels of heaven rejoice over sinners that repent, saints of God, will not you and I do the same? I do not think the church rejoices enough. We all grumble enough and groan enough, but very few of us rejoice enough. When we take a large number into the church, it is spoken of as a great mercy, but is the greatness of that mercy appreciated? I will tell you who they are that can most appreciate the conversion of sinners. They are those that are just converted themselves or those that have been great sinners themselves. Those who have been saved themselves from bondage, when they see others coming who have so lately worn the chains, are so glad that they can well take the tabret and the harp and the pipe and the psaltery and praise God that there are other prisoners who have been emancipated by grace. But there are others who can do this better still, and they are the parents and relations of those who are saved. You have thanked God many times when you have seen a sinner saved, but mother, did not you thank Him most when you saw your son converted? Oh! those holy tears; they are not tears—they are God's diamonds—the tears of a mother's joy when her son confesses his faith in Jesus. Oh! that glad countenance of the wife when she sees her husband, long bestial and drunken, at last made into a man and a Christian! Oh! that look of joy that a young Christian gives when he sees his father converted, who had long oppressed and persecuted him.

I was preaching this week for a young minister, and being anxious to know his character, I spoke of him with apparent coolness to an estimable lady of his congregation. In a very few moments she began to warm in his favor. She said, "You must not say anything against him, sir; if you do, it is because you do not know him." "Oh," I said, "I knew him long before you did; he is not much, is he?" "Well," she said, "I must speak well of him, for he has been a blessing to my servants and family." I went out into the street and saw some men and women standing about, so I said to them, "I must take your minister away." "If you do," they said, "we will follow you all over the world, if you take away a man who has done so much good to our souls." After collecting the testimony of fifteen or sixteen witnesses, I said, "If the man gets such witnesses as these, let him go on; the Lord has opened his mouth, and the devil will never be able to shut it." These are the witnesses we want—men who can sing with the angels because their own households are converted to God. I hope it may be so with all of you. If any of you are yourselves brought to Christ today—for He is willing to receive you—you will go out of this place singing, and the angels will sing with you. There shall be joy in earth and joy in heaven—on earth peace, and glory to God in the highest. The Lord bless you one and all, for Jesus' sake.

12

Satan Departing, Angels Ministering

And when the devil had ended all the temptation, he departed from him for a season (Luke 4:13).

Then the devil leaveth him, and behold, angels came and ministered unto him (Matthew 4:11).

Beloved friends, we have very much to learn from our Lord's temptation. He was tempted in all points like as we are. If you will study the temptation of Christ, you will not be ignorant of Satan's devices. If you see how He worsted the enemy, you will learn what weapons to use against your great adversary. If you see how our Lord conquers throughout the whole battle, you will learn that as you keep close to Him you will be more than conqueror through Him that loved you. From our Lord's temptation we learn especially to pray, "Lead us not into temptation." Let us never mistake the meaning of that petition. We are to pray that we may not be tempted, for we are poor flesh and blood and very frail, and it is for us to cry to God, "Lead us not into temptation." But we also learn a great deal from the close of our Lord's great threefold trial. We find Him afterward peaceful, ministered to by angels and rejoicing. That should teach us to pray, "But, if we must be tempted, deliver us from the evil," or as some render it, and very correctly, too, "Deliver us from the Evil One." First, we pray that we may not be tempted at all, and then as a supplement to that prayer, yield the whole matter to divine wisdom, "If it be needful for our manhood, for our growth in grace, for the verification of our graces, and for God's glory that we should be tempted, Lord, deliver us from the evil, and especially deliver us from the impersonation of evil, the Evil One!"

This sermon was taken from *The Metropolitan Tabernacle Pulpit* and was preached on Thursday evening, August 15, 1889.

With that as an introduction, for a short time tonight let me call upon you to notice in our text, first, *the Devil leaving the tempted One*: "Then the devil leaveth him." Secondly, we shall keep to Matthew's gospel, and notice *the angels ministering to the tempted One* after the fallen angel had left Him, and then, thirdly, *the limitation of the rest that we may expect*, the limitation of the time in which Satan will be gone, for Luke puts it, "When the devil had ended all the temptation, he departed from him *for a season*," or, as some put it, "until a fit opportunity," when he would again return, and our great Lord and Master would once more be tried by his wicked wiles.

The Devil Leaving the Tempted One

When did the Devil leave our Lord? *When he had finished the temptation.* It must have been a great relief to our divine Master when Satan left Him; the very air must have been purer and fitter to be breathed. His soul must have felt a great relief when the evil spirit had gone away, but he went not, we are told, until he had finished all the temptation. So Luke puts it: "When the Devil had ended all the temptation, he departed from him for a season." Satan will not go until he has shot the last arrow from his quiver. Such is his malice that as long as he can tempt, he will tempt. His will desires our total destruction, but his power is not equal to his will. God does not give him power such as he would like to possess; there is always a limit set to his assaults. When Satan has tempted you throughout and ended all his temptation, then he will leave you. You have not yet undergone all forms of temptation, so you may not expect absolutely and altogether to be left by the arch-enemy. It may be a long time, when you are suffering from his attacks, before he will hold his hand, for he will try all that he possibly can to lead you into evil and to destroy the grace that is in you. Still, he does come to an end with his temptations sooner than he desires, for, as God has said to the mighty sea, "Hitherto shalt thou come, but no further: and here shall thy proud waves be stayed," so says He to the Devil. When He permitted Satan to try the graces of Job and to prove his sincerity, He let him go just so far but no farther, and when he asked for a further stretch of power, still there was a limit. There is always a limit to Satan's power, and when he reaches that point he will be pulled up short; he can do no more. You are never so in the hand of Satan as to be out of the hand of God. You are never so tempted, if you are a believer, that there is not a way of escape for you. God permits you to be tried for many reasons which, perhaps, you could not altogether understand but which His infinite wisdom understands for you, but He will not suffer the rod of the wicked to rest upon the lot of the righteous. It may fall there, but it shall not rest there. The Lord may let you be put into the fire, but the fire shall be heated no hotter than you are able to bear. "When the devil had ended all the temptation, he departed from him."

Satan did not depart from Christ, however, until *he had also failed in every temptation.* When the Lord had failed him at every point, had met every temptation with a text of Holy Scripture, and had proved His own determination to hold fast His integrity and not let it go—it was not until then that the Enemy departed. Oh, brothers and sisters, if you can hold out, if you can stand against this and then against that, if you are proof against frowns and proof against flatteries, if you are proof against prosperity and proof against adversity, if you are proof against sly insinuations and open attacks, when you have won the day, as by God's grace you will do even as your Master did, then the Enemy will depart from you! "Well," says one, "I wish that he would depart from me, for I have been sorely troubled by him," to which I say most heartily, "Amen."

Let us think, for a minute or two, about when Satan will depart from the child of God as he did from the great Son of God.

I have no doubt that he will do that when he finds that it is necessary for him to be somewhere else. Satan is not everywhere and cannot be, for he is not divine. He is not omnipresent, but, as one has said, although he is not everywhere present, it would be hard to say where he is not, for he moves so swiftly; he is such an agile spirit that he seems to be here and there and everywhere. And where he is not in person, he is represented by that vast host, the legions of fallen spirits who are under his control, and even where they are not, he carries out his evil devices so that he leaves the leaven to work, the evil seeds to grow, when he himself has gone elsewhere. Yet it is, probably, not many times in one's life that any man is called actually into conflict with Satan himself personally. There are too many of us now for him to give all his time and strength to one; he has to be somewhere else. Oh, I long to be the means of multiplying the number of God's people by the preaching of the Word, that the Gospel of the grace of God may fly abroad and bring in myriads, that the Devil may have more to do and therefore not be able to give so much of his furious attention, as he does in one direction and another, to the children of God.

He also leaves God's people very quickly when he sees that they are sustained by superior grace. He hopes to catch them when grace is at a low ebb. If he can come upon them when faith is very weak, when hope's eyes are dim, when love has grown cold, then he thinks that he will make an easy capture; but where we are filled with the Spirit as the Master was—(God grant that we may be!)—he looks us up and down, and he presently sheers off, like an old pirate who hangs about on the look out for merchant vessels. But if he meets with ships that have plenty of guns on board and hardy hands to give him a warm reception, he goes after some other craft not quite so well able to resist his assaults. Oh, brothers and sisters, be not merely Christians, only barely Christians with just enough grace to let you see your imperfections, but pray to God to give you mighty grace that you may "be strong in the Lord, and in the power of his might," so that, after the Devil has tested you and found that the Lord is with you, that God dwells in you, then you may expect that, as it was with your Master, so it will be with you, Satan will leave you.

Sometimes I think, however, that Satan personally leaves us because he knows that not to be tempted is to some men a greater danger than to be tempted. "Oh!" say you, "how can that be?" Brothers, sisters, do you know nothing of carnal security, of being left, as you think, to grow in grace and to be very calm, very happy, and, as you hope, very useful and to find beneath you a sea of glass with not a ripple on the wave? "Yes," say you, "I do know that experience, and I have been thankful for it." Have you never found creeping over you at the same time the idea that you are somebody, that you are getting wonderfully experienced, that you are an eminent child of God, rich and increased in goods, and have you not said, like David, "I shall never be moved"? Possibly you have looked askance on some of your friends who have been trembling and timid and crying to God from day to day to keep them. You have been Sir Mighty; you have been Lord Great-One, and everybody must bow down before you. Ah, yes, you have now fallen into a worse condition than even those are in who are tempted of Satan! A calm in the tropics is more to be dreaded than a tempest; in such a calm everything gets to be still and stagnant; the ship scarcely moves; it is like a painted ship on a painted sea, and it gets to be in something like the state described by Coleridge's "Ancient Mariner"—

> The very deep did rot:
>   Alas, that ever this should be!
> And slimy things with legs did crawl
>   Over the slimy sea.

"Oh!" say you, "that is horrible." Yes, and that is the tendency of a soul that is at peace with itself and is not emptied from vessel to vessel. I fear that is often the case with those who believe themselves to be supernaturally holy. A curious fact can be proved by abundant evidence, namely, that the boast of human perfection is closely followed by obscenity and licentiousness. The most unclean sects that have ever defaced the page of history have been founded by those who had the notion that they were beyond temptation, that they had ceased to sin and never could transgress again. "Ah!" says Satan, "this notion does my work a great deal better than tempting a man. When I tempt him, then he stands up to resist me. He has his eyes open; he grasps his sword and puts on his helmet. He cries to God, 'Lord, help me!' and he watches night and day, and the more tempted he is, the more he looks to God for strength. But if I leave him quite alone and he goes to sleep, well then he is not in the battle, and if he begins to feel quite secure, then I can steal in upon him unawares and make a speedy end of him." This is one reason why Satan leaves some men untempted. A roaring devil is better than a sleeping devil, and there is no temptation much worse than that of never being tempted at all.

Again, I doubt not that Satan leaves us, no, I know that he does, when the Lord says to him what He said in the wilderness, "Get thee hence, Satan," and He does say that when He sees one of His poor children dragged about, tortured, wounded, bleeding. He says, "Get you hence, Satan. I permit you to fetch in my stray sheep but not to worry them to death. Get you hence, Satan." The old hell-dog knows his Master, and he flies at once.

This voice of God will come when the Lord sees that we cast ourselves wholly upon Him. In my brother's prayer he suggested to us, if you remember, that in casting our burden upon the Lord we might not be able to get rid of it; the way was to cast ourselves and our burden both upon the Lord. The best way of all is to get rid of the burden entirely, to cast yourself, but without your burden, upon the Lord. Let me remind you of a story that I once told you of a gentleman who, riding along in his gig, saw a packman carrying a heavy pack and asked him if he would like a ride. "Yes, and thank you, sir." But he kept his pack on his back while riding. "Oh!" said the friend, "why do you not take your pack off and put it down in front?" "Why, sir," he said, "it is so kind of you to give me a ride that I do not like to impose upon your good nature, and I thought that I would carry the pack myself!" "Well," said the other, "but, you see, it makes no difference to me whether you carry it or do not carry it, I have to carry you and your pack, so you had better unstrap it and put it down in front." So, friend, when you cast your burden upon God, unstrap it. Why should you bear it yourself when God is prepared to bear it? Beloved, there are times when we forget that, but when we can come and absolutely yield ourselves right up, saying, "Lord, here I am, tempted and poor and weak, but I come and rest in You. I know not what to ask at Your hands, but Your servant has said, 'Cast thy burden upon the LORD, and he shall sustain thee: he shall never suffer the righteous to be moved.' I lie at Your feet, my Lord; here I am, here would I be. Do with me as seems good in Your sight, only deal in tender mercy with Your servant," then will the Lord rebuke the Enemy; the waves of the sea shall be still, and there shall be a great calm.

So much for the Devil leaving the tempted One. He does so, he must do so, when God commands it.

The Angels Ministering to the Tempted One

The angels came and ministered to our Lord after Satan was gone. Notice that they did not come while our Lord was in the battle. Why not? Why, because it was needful that He should tread the winepress alone and because it was more glorious for Him that of the people there should be none with Him! Had there been any angels there to help Him in the duel with the adversary, they might have shared the honor of the victory, but they must stay away until the fight is over, and when the foe is gone, then the angels come. It has been noted that it does not say that the angels came very often and ministered to Jesus as much as to make us think that they were always near, that they hovered within earshot, watching and ready to interpose if they might. They were a bodyguard round about our Lord even as they are today about His people, for "are they not all ministering spirits, sent forth to minister for them who shall be heirs of salvation?" But the moment that the fight was over, then the angels came and ministered to Christ. Why was that?

I suppose, first, because as man, *He was specially exhausted.* He hungered, we are told, and that proves exhaustion, but besides that, the strain of forty days' temptation must have been immense. Men can bear up under a strain, but when it is eased, then they fall. Elijah can do marvels, he can smite the priests of Baal and behave like a hero, but after it is all over, Elijah fails. As man, our Lord was subject to the sinless infirmities of our flesh, and it was needful that angels should come and minister to Him, even as the angel did in the garden after the agony and bloody sweat.

But it was also because, being man, *He was to partake of the ministry that God had allotted to man.* He has appointed angels to watch over His own people, and inasmuch as Jesus is our Brother, as the children were partakers of the ministry of angels, He Himself also took part with the same, that He might show how He took our weakness upon Him and therefore needed and received that succor that the Father has promised to all His children.

Was it not, again, because *He was so beloved of the angels, and they were so loyal to Him?* They must have wondered when they saw Him born on earth and living here in poverty, and when they saw Him tempted of the Enemy, they must have loathed the adversary. How could Satan be permitted to come so near their pure and holy Master? I think that Milton could have pictured this scene and that he would have drawn every seraph there as longing to let his falchion of flame find a scabbard in the heart of the foul fiend that dared to come so near to the Prince of purity, but they must not interfere. Yet as soon as ever they might, then they joyfully came and ministered to Him.

And does it not also go to show that *His was a nature very sensitive to the angelic touch?* You and I are coarse, hardhearted.

> Myriads of spirits throng the air:
> They are about us now.

Women are to cover their heads in worship "because of the angels." There are many acts of decorum in holy worship that are to be kept up "because of the angels." They are innumerable; they are sent to minister to us, but we are not sentient to them; often we do not perceive them. But Jesus was all tenderness and sensitiveness, and He knew that the angels were there, so it was easy for them to come and minister to Him. What they did in ministering to Him we cannot tell. I should certainly think that they sustained His bodily nature, for He hungered, and they readily brought to Him food, but they also sustained His mental and His spiritual nature with words of comfort. The sight of them reminded Him of His Father's house, reminded Him of the glory that He had laid aside. The sight of them proved that the Father did not forget Him. He had sent the household troops of heaven to succor and support Him. The sight of them must have made Him anticipate the day of which the poet sings,

> They brought his chariot from above,
> To bear him to his throne;
> Clapp'd their triumphant wings, and cried,
> "The glorious work is done."

Well now, brethren, if we are tempted, shall we have any angels to succor us? Well, we shall have the equivalent of angels, certainly. Oftentimes, after a temptation, God sends His human messengers. Many of you can tell how, when you have been hearing the Word after a bad time of temptation, the Gospel message has been wonderfully sweet to you. You have sat in your pew and said, "God sent that sermon on purpose for me," or, if you have not had a sermon, you have read the Bible, and the words have seemed to burn and glow on the page, and you have warmed your soul by their heat. Has it not been so with you often? Are not all the holy things more sweet after trial than they were before? Have you not found them so? I bear my willing witness that never does Christ seem so precious, never do the promises seem so rich and rare, never does evangelical doctrine cling so closely to my heart, and my heart to it, as after a time of painful trial when I have been laid aside from holy service and racked with anguish. Oh, then the angels come and minister to us in the form of men who preach the Word or in the form of the living page of God's written Word!

I have noticed, too, that God sometimes cheers His tempted people with clear sunshine after rain by some very gracious providences. Something happens that they could not have looked for, so pleasant, so altogether helpful that they have had to burst into singing, though just before they had been sighing. The cage door was set wide open, and God's bird has had such a flight and sung so sweetly as it mounted up to heaven's gate that the soul seemed transformed into a holy lark in its ascending music. Have you not found the Lord very gracious to you after some severe trial or some strong temptation? I believe that this will be the testimony of many experienced Christians.

And as there come these choice providences, so I do not doubt there do come actual angels ministering to us, though we are unaware of their presence. They can suggest holy thoughts, I doubt not, to bring us comfort, but above the angels, far superior to angelic help, is the Holy Spirit the Comforter. How sweetly can He close up every wound and make it even sing as it heals! He makes the bones that God had broken to rejoice and fills us with a deeper experience of delight than we have ever known before.

Well now, I suppose that some of you here tonight are in this condition that Satan has left you and angels are ministering to you. If so, you are very happy. Bless your God for it. There is a great calm. Thank God for the calm after the storm. I hope, my brother, that you are the stronger for what you have endured and that the conflict has matured you and prepared you for something better. Now, what did our Lord do after the Devil had left Him and the angels had come to minister to Him? Did He go home and stop there and begin to sing of His delightful experiences? No, we find Him preaching directly afterward, full of the Spirit of God. He went everywhere proclaiming the kingdom. He was found in the synagogue or on the hillside. Just in proportion as the Spirit of God had enabled Him to overcome the Enemy, we find Him going forth to spend that strength in the service of His Lord. O tempted one, have you a respite? Spend that respite for Him who gave it to you. Is it calm now after a storm? Go now, and sow your fields with the good seed. Have you wiped your eye, and is the salt tear gone? Go you, sing a psalm, then; sing to your well-beloved; go you down to His vineyard and take the foxes and prune the vines and dig about them and do necessary work for Him who has done so much for you. Listen. You have been set free. There are many under bondage to Satan, not as you are, fighting against him, but his willing slaves. Oh, come my brother, your God has set you free, go after them! Go after the fallen woman and the drunken man. Go, seek and find the most debauched, the most depraved. Specially look after any of your own house who have played the prodigal.

> Oh, come, let us go and find them!
> In the paths of death they roam:
> At the close of the day 'twill be sweet to say,
> "I have brought some lost one home."

And it will be right to say it, if the Lord has dealt so well with thee.

The Limitation of Rest

Did the Devil assail our Lord again? I am not sure that he personally did, but he did so in divers ways by others. I notice that before long he tried to entangle Him in His speech. That is a very easy thing to do with us. Somebody tonight can take up something that I have said, twist it from its connection, and make it sound and seem totally different from what was meant by it. You know how the Herodians, the Sadducees, and the Pharisees did this with our Lord; they tried to entangle Him in His speech. In all that, Satan led them on. Satan also actively opposed Christ's ministry, and Christ opposed Satan—but Jesus won the day, for He saw Satan fall like lightning from heaven.

A more artful plan still was that by which the Devil's servants, the demons that were cast out of possessed persons, called Jesus the Son of God. He rebuked them because He did not want any testimony from them. No doubt the Devil thought it a very cunning thing to praise the Savior because then the Savior's friends would begin to be suspicious of Him, if He was praised by the Devil. This was a deep trick, but the Master made him hold his peace. You remember how He said on one occasion, "Hold thy peace, and come out of him." It was something like this, "Down dog! Come out!" Christ is never very polite with Satan; a few words, and very strong ones, are all that are necessary for this arch-prince of wickedness.

Satan tempted our Lord through Peter. That is a plan that he has often tried with us—setting a friend of ours to do his dirty work. Peter took his Lord and rebuked Him when He spoke about being spit upon and put to death, and then the Lord said, "Get thee behind me, Satan!" He could see the Devil using Peter's tenderness to try to take Him off from His self-sacrifice. Oh, how often has Satan tempted us that way, entangling us in our speech, opposing us in our work, praising us out of wicked motives to try to deceive us, and then setting some friend to try to take us off from holy self-denial!

There were also occasional heart-sinkings in our Lord. Thus we read in John 12:27, "Now is my soul troubled; and what shall I say? Father, save me from this hour." He seems to have been very heavy in heart at that time. But the deepest soul-sinking was when in the garden His soul was "exceeding sorrowful, even unto death." Satan had a hand in that sore trial, for the Lord had said, "The prince of this world cometh," and He said to those who came to arrest Him, "This is your hour, and the power of darkness." It was a dreadful season. Our Lord's ministry began and ended with a fierce onslaught from Satan. He left Him after the temptation, but only for a season.

Well now, dear friends, if we have peace and quietness tonight and are not tempted, do not let us become self-secure. The Devil will come to us again at a fit opportunity. And when will that be? There are a great many fit opportunities with you and with me. One is *when we have nothing to do.* You know Dr. Watts' lines—

> Satan finds some mischief still,
> For idle hands to do.

He will come and attack us *when we are alone*; I mean, when we are sad and lonely and are sitting still and moping by ourselves.

But Satan also finds a very fit occasion *when we are in company*, especially when it is very mixed company, a company of persons, perhaps, who are superior to us in education and in station but who do not fear God. We may easily be overawed and led astray by them. Satan will come then.

I have known him frequently come and find an occasion against the children of God *when we are sick and ill*, the old coward! He knows that we would not mind him when we are in good health, but sometimes when we are down in the dumps through sickness and pain, then it is that he begins to tempt us to despair.

So will he do with us *when we are very poor.* When a man has had a great loss in business, down comes Satan and insinuates, "Is *this* how God treats His children? God's people are no better off than other people."

Then, *if we are getting on in the world*, he turns it the other way, and he says, "Does Job fear God for nothing? He gets on by his religion." You cannot please the Devil anyhow, and you need not want to please him; he can make a temptation for you out of anything.

I am going to say something that will surprise you. One time of great temptation is *when we are very spiritual.* As to myself, I have never been in such supreme danger as when I have led some holy meeting with sacred fervor and have felt carried away with delight in God. You know that it is easy to be on the Mount of Transfiguration and then to meet Satan at the foot, as our Lord did when He came down from that hill.

Another time of temptation is *when we have already done wrong.* "Now he begins to slip," says Satan, "I saw him trip. Now I will have him down." Oh, for speedy repentance and an earnest flight to Christ whenever there has been a grave fault, aye, and before the grave fault comes, that we may be preserved from falling!

And Satan finds a good occasion for tempting us *when we have not sinned.* After we have been tempted and we have won the day and stood fast, then he comes and says, "Now, that was well done on your part; you are a splendid saint." He who thinks himself a splendid saint is next door to a shameful sinner, depend upon it, and Satan soon gets the advantage over him.

If you are successful in business or successful in holy work, then Satan will tempt you. If you are not successful in holy work, then Satan will tempt you. If you are not successful and have had a bad time, then Satan will tempt you. When you have a heavy load to carry, he will tempt you. When that load is taken off, then he will tempt you worse than ever. He will tempt you when you have obtained some blessing that you have been thinking was such a great blessing—just as in the wilderness when they would cry for flesh and said that they must have flesh, God gave them their heart's desire "but sent leanness into their soul." Just as you have secured the thing that you are seeking, then comes a temptation, to which all I have to say is this: Watch. "What I say unto you I say unto all. Watch," said Christ. Watch and pray, that ye enter not into temptation." And by the conflict and the victory of your Master, go into the conflict bravely and expect to conquer by faith in Him, even as He overcame.

But what shall I say to those who are the slaves and the friends of Satan? The Lord have mercy upon you! If you desire to escape, there is only one way. There is the cross, and Christ does hang upon it. Look to Jesus; He can set you free. He came on purpose to proclaim liberty to the captives. Look and live. Look now, and live now. I implore you do it for His dear sake. Amen.